Creative
Pastoral Management

by
Roy E. Carnahan

Beacon Hill Press of Kansas City
Kansas City, Missouri

Copyright, 1976
Beacon Hill Press of Kansas City

ISBN: 0-8341-0441-5

Printed in the
United States of America

Creative

Pastoral

Management

Contents

Foreword

The vision of distinguished service to God and man challenges every real pastor. Our pastoral labors, the most important caring relationship known to man, carry a gigantic price tag—our lives. But abundantly rich rewards come to those who pastor well. Jesus promised, "He that loses his life . . . shall find it." And how accurate He was!

In *Creative Pastoral Management,* Roy E. Carnahan —both a dreamer and a doer—shares his long experience and serious thoughts. His whole ministry has been shaped by an eagerness to do better today than he did yesterday—and those who know him well thought yesterday was pretty good. His ideas are demanding and dynamic too. These concepts cry out to be tried today—**NOW.**

PALCON, Pastors Leadership Conferences—a giant step forward in renewal and pastoral development by the Church of the Nazarene—presents *Creative Pastoral Management* to every Nazarene pastor with a prayerful hope that your pastoral management will make your church flourish like a spring dandelion.

—Neil B. Wiseman
Director, PALCON, 1976

Preface

My interest in church management developed soon after I accepted my first pastoral charge, a home mission church in Potsdam, N.Y. We began with new Nazarenes and a few converts. Since there were no management precedents, I had to develop administrative leadership through trial and error—a good many errors.

My second assignment was a new church, Rochester East Side. This congregation included a few charter member Nazarenes from other churches. After more than two years, this church was merged with another congregation to become Rochester Calvary Church. I served this congregation for more than 10 years. The lay leaders there worked closely with me in the constant development of administrative procedures. It was there that I developed most of my basic concepts for control forms, job descriptions, and long-range planning.

During these 13 years in Rochester, I served with various religious organizations outside the local church and had opportunity to observe the leadership styles of successful Christian workers. At Rochester Calvary Church, I left behind a complete management manual called *Standard Practice*.

My next pastorate was Baltimore First Church. Here I found very capable laymen and the legacy of good pastoral leadership. Baltimore First Church had many well-established operating policies which I combined with my Rochester experience, and a new *Standard Practice* was developed. A copy of *Standard Practice* stayed in the church office when I resigned. My successor indicated that this manual made the pastoral leadership transition much easier.

After being elected district superintendent of the Washington District, I began to share with my pastors this *Standard Practice* which had been developed over 18 years. I discovered that poor management techniques and faulty leadership have been barriers to the growth of many local churches.

Several people have helped develop my management concepts. The late Paul E. Wells, an accountant, district treasurer, and at one time business manager of Eastern Nazarene College, helped me see how certain bookkeeping practices could be used in church administration. John H. Golden, presently a Du Pont plant manager, a close personal friend since college days, and once my Sunday school superintendent, helped me to understand the importance of sound church management principles. James A. Jackson, my father-in-law, with many years of management experience with Eastman Kodak Company, gave me the idea of writing *Standard Practice*.

I also want to recognize the impact on me of "Men in Action," led by Terry Gyger. They developed a comprehensive program of local church evangelism and administration. Their evangelism instruction has given rise to "Nazarenes in Action," a program that is being increasingly used in our denomination. Their management instruction helped me to organize my thoughts and has had great influence in the development of this book.

It is my desire that this book will help pastors better understand church management and give them some administrative aids to make their work more effective.

Roy E. Carnahan

Chapter 1

CHURCH MANAGEMENT
A SKILL TO BE DEVELOPED

No one builds a church in his own strength. But our Lord promised, "I will build my church, and the gates of Hades will not overcome it" (Matt. 16:18, NIV). And history supports His claim. For 2,000 years the Church of Jesus Christ has grown in spite of violent hostility from the world and the frequent failure of church members. The history of the Church testifies to its own supernatural character; it has been blessed by God as a persistently overcoming institution. Even when faced by overwhelming obstacles, continual renewal has come from within the Church itself through believers who through the enablement of the Holy Spirit, minister to others.

Who Builds the Church?

God constructs the Church, but men are always God's instruments for extending it. Since He works through people to accomplish His purpose, we can be confident that God wants to build the Church through people like us. It is the pastor's task to provide a faithful human channel through which God may extend His Church.

What Is the Church?

Pastors are frequently pulled in different directions and frustrated by the numerous demands made on them by their congregations and communities. As a pastor who takes his work seriously, you search for better ways to do your work—ways that are consistent with New Testament principles and relevant to twentieth-century people. Frustrations are lessened and effectiveness increased when a pastor sees a basic unity in his work. Such unity helps a minister decide what must be done in a given time frame and in what priority.

Both the interrelatedness and the wholeness of the pastor's work is seen in the five basic functions of the church's ministry, which are: (1) worship; (2) evangelism; (3) disciplining; (4) fellowship; and (5) mercy. A proper view of these ministries provides a giant first step to awareness which is so essential for a purposeful and sustained ministry in a church and to a community. After establishing such an overview unity, a pastor is ready to think about church growth and his part in it.

Kinds of Growth

As in the realm of nature, so in the church—wherever there is life, there will be growth. Life in our human bodies produces continual renewal; and while that growth is not always evident, eventually it becomes obvious. Likewise we may expect to see growth in the body of Christ.

In his church growth lectures, Donald McGavran insists that church development appears in three areas: quantitatively, qualitatively, and organically.

Quantitative growth, usually the most evident, shows when the church is spiritually alive. Within a reasonable amount of time, there will be more people in it. Because people are its main business, we are concerned about increased attendance and membership. Living churches produce increasing membership rolls.

Qualitative growth, though more subtle, is equally essential. Such qualitative growth produces in believers increased evidence of the nature of Christ. This shows itself in a deepening of devotion, greater faith in prayer, greater love for the Bible, stability in doctrine, and obedience to God's leadership.

Organic growth means that every member is experiencing his own gift and practising his unique ministry. Organic growth is seen when members consider themselves ministers of Jesus Christ and actively engage themselves in meaningful ministries. This is the realization that the gifts of the Spirit (Eph. 4:11-12) given to all Christians are to be used to build the Church and do God's work on earth.

All three—quantitative, qualitative, and organic growth—are necessary to make the Church the dynamic, living organism God planned it to be.

God's ultimate purpose in this world is to build His Church. Note the biblical references to the Church as the body of Christ: Rom. 12:5; Cor. 12:27; Eph. 1:23; 4:12; Col. 1:24; 2:19. God is building His Church in the world. And to be a part of this divine building process provides a lifelong challenge for the Christian leader. Is there any greater use for life than to contribute to the building of Christ's Church?

Jesus' Work Continued

Acts 1:1 states, "The former treatise have I written, O Theophilus, *of all that Jesus began both to do and teach.*" The inference is clear. Christ only *began* His earthly ministry. The record of Early Church development after His departure follows in these first chapters of Acts. But Pentecost was only the beginning of the Church. The work goes on. Since then the Holy Spirit continues the ministry of Jesus by purifying lives for a holy relationship with God and empowering them for service through he church. Thus the church has become the divine instrument to continue the work Jesus started.

If one is searching for a mission for the church in any community, he might very well start by asking, "What would Jesus do if He were here?" The answer becomes the mandate of the church in every location. Of course, we cannot duplicate Christ's great ministry on Calvary as an atonement for sin. But all of His ministries involving help to people serve as a pattern for our ministry today.

The church because of its task to continue this ministry of Christ in the world takes predominance over all the other institutions. There is no higher calling than to be a pastor who leads believers in their ministry among men.

The Role of a Pastor in Church Growth

Paul, the church builder, clarified leadership roles the church as follows: "It was he who gave some to be apostles, some to be prophets, some to be evangelists and some to be pastors and teachers, to prepare God's people for works of service, so that the body of Christ may be built up" (Eph. 4:11-12, NIV). God pro-

14

vides four kinds of ministries in order to build His Church.

He first sent *apostles.* These were men who had come to know Jesus in this earthly life, believed, became His followers, and were then commissioned to go into their communities to preach the Good News. They were the human founders of the Church, and their credibility was based on their personal witness of the Resurrection. They performed a unique, never-to-be repeated function at the outset of the Church.

Prophets were also given to the Church as forth-tellers of the Word of God. These men could not take gospel texts and preach as we do because the New Testament was not yet available. God communicated directly to them, and they relayed His message to their communities through preaching. Now we have both the Old and New Testaments as God's complete Revelation, so the present-day prophet, like the ancient town crier, announces the truth of the Scriptures.

The *evangelists* come next in the Ephesian listing. These were God's servants with special gifts in effective proclamation of the gospel to unsaved people; they lead hearers to conversion. In God's army these are the front-line warriors, the shock troops who first invade enemy territory to liberate the captives and make spiritual beachheads. Pioneer missionaries and home mission evangelists are probably the best examples of the New Testament evangelists. This is a special kind of ministry which is absolutely essential to the ongoing of the church. Ideally, the evangelist is one who ministers outside the church. If God has given the evangelism gift to certain individuals, they need to be released to work in the world proclaiming the gospel to the unsaved. The evangelist's work inside the church is successful only as the church gets the unsaved people inside the church building.

As a ministry which follows the work of apostles, prophets and evangelists, there must be a great host of *pastors*. These persons are gifted to edify the church and lead it into useful ministry. The term *pastor* is equated with the biblical word which is translated "shepherd" *(poimen)*. It is assumed that there are converts, either as the result of the ministry of the evangelist or of church members involved in evangelism. Now these converts must be fed, nurtured, instructed, encouraged, directed, edified, and put to work for Christ.

The pastor is also overseer or bishop *(episkopos)*. If spiritual declension has set in on the church, the pastor must lead in the ministry of revival. Revival assumes there has been life that has either diminished or died and that must once again be renewed. Revival is basically directed to the spiritual decline of church members and to backsliders. Essentially the pastor's role is the ministry of challenge, rebuke and exhortation.

There is also the sense in which the pastor is involved in evangelism, as indicated by the words of Paul to Timothy, "Do the work of an evangelist" (2 Tim. 4:5). Thus the ministries of pastor and evangelist cannot be divorced. However, most ministers are more gifted in one or the other. We also recognize that all Christians are evangelists in a basic sense.

Management Defined

What is management? George R. Terry and Roger H. Hermanson suggest that management deals with achievement by individuals contributing their best efforts in accordance with predetermined actions.[1]

16

Basically a manager is an overseer. This function is absolutely necessary for the church and the edification of believers who comprise the church. And this implies that the leader knows what should be done, knows how it should be done, understands how to get people to do it, and evaluates the overall effectiveness of what is done. The pastor is that kind of overseer of the people of God. What an honor it is to be an overseer of God's work in His forever family on earth.

Presently there is an unfortunate misunderstanding of the pastor's role. Too frequently he is considered an employee of the church—the "super" saint hired to do the work of the ministry in a particular congregation. He is the professional Christian. It is even possible the pastor may hold this concept of himself.

But the manager-overseer could never stoop to be a hireling. He is a shepherd—a leader who gladly spends his life for the noble task. He has no time for trivia. The real pastor seeks to continually update his leadership skills for greater effectiveness.

Biblical Management Skills Explained

Every pastor has either a potential or developed gift of an overseeing ministry. Frequently persons are considered for a pastorate purely on the basis of their call to preach. But this overseeing ministry, while it involves preaching, is much more. Our churches need pastors who can effectively manage the church. When we consider licensing or ordaining a man to the ministry, we must look for evidence of his pastoral, overseeing potential and his managerial gifts.

While we do not discount the multitalented person who is able to do many things well and is a great motivator of people, we recognize that this is not essen-

17

tially the biblical idea of a pastor. There are relatively few people who have such outstanding abilities. There simply are not enough such leaders to do the job throughout the world. God's plan is to enable ordinary people to achieve extraordinary feats in building His Church. But what are the needed skills and how do we develop them?

Look again at the Bible in Eph. 4:12. Here is found clear evidence of the skills needed for pastoral ministry. First, he is an *equipper* of the saints. The saints, obviously, are the people of God who make up the body of Christ. Paul uses *katartismon* here, which means setting a dislocated bone. Additional word meanings suggest bringing together opposing factions or refitting a ship to make it seaworthy. In Mark 1:19, the word refers to mending of nets. Again the word appears in Gal. 6:11 where disciplining an offending church member makes him again fit for the fellowship of the church. Basically the equipping idea means to put a person or a thing into the condition for which it was origianlly intended.

The pastor must also be an *engager*—a recruiter who enlists workers for the church's ministry. The enormous task of the Church to win the world for Christ necessarily implies the involvement of the people of God *(laos)*, commonly called the laity. Because of where they work and live, their efforts are usually more effective than the pastor's. His contacts with the world are limited; theirs, nearly limitless. The unconverted expect the professional minister to do God's work, but they are more impressed when they see ordinary church members without official religious office ministering and evangelizing. The laity are never mere submissive members of a congregation who are expected simply to pay the bills. Rather they must be led into the total task of evangelism, teaching, and service.

So the people of God must be mobilized into meaningful ministeries. Such must go beyond routine tasks. Like the minister, laymen have the gifts of wisdom, prophecy, exhortation, and teaching. They must be recruited and led to strengthen the church by the effective use of their gifts.

Then, too, the Scriptures teach that the pastor is to be the *edifier* of the church. The pastor gives attention to the spiritual development of the entire body. He must give pastoral care to each individual. In Christ's stead he helps the hurting. The pastor shows concern for unity. He will seek, lead, organize, and correlate individual ministries so that they mesh together in an effective organization. He studies and preaches the Word of God to feed the people—sound doctrine must be taught. He must pray and intercede for them. Although he is not the congregation's errend boy, he builds a serving style of ministry like the towel incident from the ministry of Jesus.

As edifier, the pastor seriously works to encourage, develop, and build up the people who compose the Church. He knows the spiritual quality of their lives largely determines their effectiveness. Through this effort the body of Christ is healthy and vigorous—happy Christians doing God's work in the world.

In reality, pastors should be the world's best managers, for they have oversight of the most important of all organizations.

Secular Versus Church Management

Management leads the people of God to the best use of their human abilities, financial resources, facilities, ideas, and the grace of God. Actually it is a guardianship given to the pastor by God, by the church, and by the people. The question is not the survival of the church but the quality of its service for Christ to people. The term "church manager" implies no secularization of pastoral ministry. Neither does it infer that the work of management in some way replaces the gifts of the Spirit for the edification of the church. But there are certain parallels between the work of a pastor and the manager of a business.

How can pastors better understand these similarities and make the most of them? Giving attention to management principles is no different than the person with musical gifts taking organ lessons in order to be able to play better for the church services. Pastors improve their management skills in order to provide additional means through which the Holy Spirit may work.

As noted above, the Bible calls the pastor an overseer (Acts 20:28). This work of overseeing is vital to any organization and especially the church. The pastor is more likely to reach New Testament objectives when he uses good management principles in working with his people. The pastor must understand that he is as much a minister when he is involved in management as when he is calling or preaching. Since many pastors have no management training, they find it easier to concentrate on teaching, visiting, or counselling. Action work is more appealing to many pastors than the less spectacular task of working through others—training them for service. Action often brings immediate results but may not produce the same long-run effectiveness that would have come through better management.

Management has been defined as getting things done through other people. Church management is generally divided into four categories: *planning, leading, organizing,* and *controlling.* It must be seen as a specific, identifiable work, requiring tools and skills. Management aids include job descriptions, statements of purpose, policies, and organizational charts. W. F. Bryan Says, "There are some things God will bless as a supplement that He will curse as a substitute."[2] Management skills can never replace the impact of spiritual power made possible by the Holy Spirit but there need be no conflict.

Leadership—Natural or Developed

The most common misconception is that good leadership requires a strong, natural leader—one with charisma. Such a leader is frequently effective but usually for a relatively short period of time. Nonetheless, the natural leader possesses positive qualities useful in some specific situations. Frequently his efforts are needed in pioneer work. He may also be effective where there are special problems and a "heavy hand" is temporarily needed.

But the church cannot build on only a few strong, natural leaders. For His own purpose God has called thousands of less spectacular persons into pastoral service. Such pastors can have an effective ministry and with the development of management skills will have solid, long-range effectiveness.

Every God-called pastor, whether a strong, natural leader or not, has a place of useful service which can be greatly multiplied with a thorough understanding of management skills. Every pastor can build stronger Christians and develop great churches by employing these techniques.

Chapter 2

PLANNING—FOUNDATION OF CHURCH MANAGEMENT

"The difference between the church that does everything decently and in order and the confused, disturbed church is due largely to Spirit-led planning" is the way Gaines S. Dobbins explains the need for planning.[1] It is an important prerequisite for all successful enterprises, but planning takes hard work.

Congregations listen to a pastor preach or lead a service, and they are impressed with his performance. But often these same people do not see or value the planning that goes on before an event. But lack of planning lowers most church efforts to a level of mediocrity. Planning requires great personal discipline and often huge amounts of time from decision makers.

Planning, to be effective, follows prayer. In fact, prayer stimulates planning. Prayer seeks out God's will on a question. Then our planning organizes our steps to accomplish His purpose. It is an obvious principle that any desired future achievement is more likely to occur when prayer and planning are systematically applied to the attainment of the goal.

Planning requires decision before actions. This process involves gathering pertinent information, making reasonable assumptions, identifying possible problems, and stating expected outcomes. Since progress always requires change, the planner expects change and tries to anticipate the way people will react to it. Planning, like the study of a map, is required before taking a trip into an unknown territory.

The planner is tomorrow-minded. Planning is predetermining a course of action. After prayer and knowing what ought to be done, the pastor plans by arranging all the ingredients for success in priority order. He seeks to determine future events rather than allowing them to just happen.

Of course uncertainty of the future makes planning complicated. Often there is no previous experience, precedent, or model. Therefore since planning requires hard work and deals with uncertainties, leaders turn to the less fatiguing work of physical activity. Or worse they give in to the unproductive course of unquestioned tradition.

Due to lack of imagination, initiative, and courage to innovate, pastors may be tempted to completely bypass planning. But every pastor must face the inevitable fact that plans (or lack of plans) today will determine both the action and achievement of tomorrow.

Short- and Long-term Planning

Planning must include both short term and long term. Long-term plans help to clarify the end results we hope to accomplish. Short-term plans outline the activities necessary to accomplish the long-range plans. The pastor, because he has oversight of the entire local church, must have plans which are inclusive enough to take in all functions of the church's mission. And in this overall plan, he needs a long-range projection.

A successful business executive recently presented a large notebook to his board of directors which was approximately one inch thick and contained his proposed long-range plans. The long-range plan included a statement of ultimate goals. This plan notebook covered 10 years. After reviewing this first book, he presented a second notebook which was approximately three inches thick. This larger book contained his short-range plan for the immediate year. Before taking 10 steps, the leader must first take 1. His short-range book contained elaborate details as to how the corporation should function immediately in order to move towards the overall goals.

Every church needs both long- and short-range plans.

The church's short-range plans should show how it proposes to worship, evangelize, disciple, fellowship, and demonstrate its social or community concerns ("show mercy") this year, and what it must do immediately to move toward fulfilling its potential in these five ingredients of church life.

The long-range church plans should consider the maximum ministry of the church in a stipulated period of time in the light of the condition of the world and the church. They are, of course, subject to change as an update of goals or procedures becomes necessary. It is not as important that the church actually accomplish the specific, long-range plan as it is to always have a long-range plan before it to give direction to what it does now. It is conceivable that a church in a 10-year planning program may experience unforeseen change that would require a complete alteration of the long-rang plan after 2 or 3 years. Perhaps the long-range goals may not have been realistic, and after a few years it is evident that they should be decreased or enlarged. Thus a church need not stay rigidly with a 10-year plan but be free to make changes and set up new goals.

Basil S. Walsh advises:

> An intelligent plan is a first step to success. The man who plans knows where he is going, knows what progress he is making, and has a pretty good idea when he will arrive. Planning is the open road to your destination. If you don't know where you are going, how can you expect to get there?[2]

Recently the *Sheraton Park Hotel News* summarized the need for planning in these words: "People don't plan to fail—they just fail to plan."[3]

The Ingredients of Planning

Fayol outlines in simple form the essential steps in planning as follows: "The plan of action is at one and the same time the results envisaged, the line of action to be followed, the stages to go through, and the methods to use."[4] Items involved in planning include:

1. STATEMENT OF PURPOSE. The most important phase of planning is a clear understanding and statement of the purpose for the church's existence. No plan can be adequate until the purpose is clearly defined.

2. GOALS AND OBJECTIVES. After the purpose is stated, cite goals and objectives which, when reached, will fulfill the stated purpose.

3. FORECASTING. Planning must include an estimate of what the future will be like. This will determine all of the other remaining items of planning.

4. **PROGRAMMING.** Any outline of action with sequence is a program. Programs may be simple or complex, but achievement requires an establishment of priority of activities and actions.

5. **SCHEDULING.** Program planning must consider the time element. Scheduling is simply attaching the time frame to the plans.

6. **BUDGETING.** This must be thought of in broader terms than just money. Budgeting must be seen as a gathering and making available of *all* resources, including money, people, talents, equipment, and facilities.

7. **PROCEDURES.** This is an outline of how to do specified work. It is detailed, carefully thought out, and specifies all that is necessary to accomplish a function.

8. **POLICIES.** A policy is best understood as a standing answer to recurring questions. Policies anticipate problems of a regular nature. Policies save time by making decisions before the routine problem occurs.

Statement of Purpose

In church management seminars, when the ministers are asked to state the goals of their churches, there is usually quite a variety of statements. It is rather apparent, also, that most churches do not have stated goals. The confusion relates to the fact that there is no clear statement of purpose. As important as goals are, they cannot be established without a clear statement of purpose. At this point in the pastors' seminars, goal setting is usually abandoned and a discussion or purpose begins.

The purpose of the church must be clearly defined,

understood, and accepted by all of its lay leaders. The purpose simply states the reason for its existence. For the church, the statement of purpose is basically the same everywhere. Goals and objectives may change with conditions, but the purpose of the church, as stated in the Scriptures, is constant and universal. Such a statement might read: *The purpose of the church is to glorify God by making disciples of all nations through the continued ministry of Jesus in worship, evangelism, discipleship, fellowship, and mercy.*

The purpose must be broad enough to include every action in which the church is involved. This statement of purpose sits in judgment over every action and activity in church life and expresses the organization's continued reason for existence.

Setting Goals and Objectives

Early in the planning process but following a precise statement of purpose and a careful study of the present status of the church, the pastor, as a manager of the church, should lead the way in setting goals and objectives. Although the church board or other decision-making groups participate in this phase, the pastor must take the initiative.

Goals express what the organization wants to accomplish. They define what the church will look like when it is effective. As pointed out earlier, the church may have several goals, both of long- and short-range duration. When a goal is reached, it may be replaced with larger goals. It is likely that the church's goals will change from year to year.

Objectives are statements expressing what we propose to do in order to reach our goals. Thus the church should have many objectives. These are usually short-range and may change as soon as specific levels are reached.

Steps in Planning

The manager must first identify the purpose of the church, then state what the church hopes to accomplish (goals), and finally outline steps (objectives) toward the achievement of those goals. His focus will always be on objectives rather than obstacles.

The purpose states "Why." The goals state "What." The objectives state "Where," "When," and "How."

Catchy themes, mottoes, and generalizations can never take the place of clear-cut objectives. Many good ideas fail because they have not been made specific and reachable by definite goals and objectives. Leaders often make the mistake of trying to motivate people with rallying calls which lack a statement of precise action. The people do not respond because they do not know what actions to take. The leader may say, "Let's do something;" but unless he further defines what needs doing, achievements are doubtful.

The sighting of goals and objectives helps to identify the results to be accomplished through purposeful action. Mere activity without attention to purpose seldom produces desirable ends. The trend is to lose sight of goals and have only activities. Churches generally have a clear concept of purpose in their beginning days. However, with the passing of time, the increasing preoccupation with activities, the erosion of the world, the death or moving away of original members, or spiritual decline, the church's emphasis tends to shift from specific goals to maintenance operations. A church is in decline when it finds pleasure only in the routine operations.

28

Objectives must be definitive so as to set boundaries; they must be measurable with quantitative values. They deal with how many, how big, and when. These serve as bench marks to measure the church's progress in its mission for Christ.

Goals and objectives need to be reasonable and within the ability of the group to achieve. They need to be demanding enough to inspire the church to do its best. Motivation is inherent in challenging goals.

Goals become personalized by involving the entire group in their formation. This is accomplished when the pastor involves the church board and other committees in setting the goals. For example, when a pastor sets a goal to receive 25 members on profession of faith within a certain period of time but does not involve lay leaders in formulating plans to accomplish this, the people may expect the pastor to "Go ahead and do it." People work harder for goals over which they feel some sense of ownership.

Having too many goals will scatter interest. A few well-chosen ones will help focus efforts on specific results. Goals should produce concentrated effort.

If the purpose of the church is to "glorify God by making disciples of all people through the continued ministry of Jesus in worship, evangelism, discipleship, fellowship, and mercy," or, more simply, to please God, then some worthy annual goals might be to have 25 new members by profession of faith, increase the giving of the church by 10 percent, have a net membership increase of 35, and pay off the mortgage by March 31. (The size of the goals is somewhat controlled by the size and condition of the church.) Below these stated goals the objectives may be: to present the plan of salvation in 100 homes this year, to conduct two evangelistic crusades, to preach a series of four sermons on Christian stewardship in February, to raise a building fund pledge of $10,000, and to train 10 people in personal evangelism. Notice these goals and objectives are definitive, measurable, and have inspiration potential. And when accomplished, they fulfill the stated purpose of the church.

Worthwhile goals and objectives will prompt and inspire the people to work in the ministry of the church. It is a well-known principle that "it is better to put 10 men to work than to try to do the work of 10 men."

Robert Townsend, when president of Avis Corporation, was strong on having clearly defined goals. Several staff members spent months identifying the company's goal which was finalized as: "We want to become the fastest growing company with the highest profit margin in the business of renting and leasing vehicles without drivers."[5] These 23 words helped the Avis Corporation to concentrate on objectives and rise to new business success.

The same principle—clear, concise, achievable goals owned and easily understood by the people—will have the same positive results in the church. Many churches could show greater growth if the pastor, as the manager of God's people, would lead his congregation into the formulation and adoption of specific goals.

Forecasting

Forecasting means having a fairly accurate estimate of what future conditions will be. Ingredients of forecasting include sociological, economic, educational, geographic, political, and social trends. In order for the church to perform its ministry, it must be able to understand its environment.

One of the most dangerous examples of poor forecasting is the assumption that tomorrow will be an uninterrupted extension of today. Change is happening at an ever increasing rate. Pastors might well keep alert to sociological trends. One recent significant book is Alvin Toffler's *Future Shock.* If Mr. Toffler is right, the shape and program of tomorrow's churches will need to be considerably altered if they are to have meaning on the contemporary scene.

The church must know its community if it is to plan programs that will meet the needs of its prospects. It needs sociological information. Resources, both people and money, are very easily wasted on inappropriate programs based on suppositions which are not based on factual data. Forecasting must consider the schedules and working conditions of the people. The timing of services should be designed to meet the changing schedules of people. The kind of people who live near a church should help determine the types of services a church offers.

Since structures of brick and mortar are difficult to move and expensive to alter, effective forecasting is especially necessary when a church considers a building project. In good forecasting, the planning committee must also consider what kind of people will probably populate the neighborhood in future years. Will the neighborhood be largely of youth or older people, be wealthy or indigent, have ethnic concentrations, be church oriented or unchurched? Also the proximity of colleges, grade schools, industry, and the availability of transportation should be considered.

Forecasting requires the observation of community business trends. Conferences with Chamber of Commerce personnel plus a review of their literature often proves beneficial in forecasting.

Programming

Programming is the sequence or the priority of necessary steps to accomplish the objectives and goals. Any action resulting from planning produces a program. For example, the Sunday morning order of service is a program. The order of service has a great deal to do with the effectiveness of worship.

Since the church has many goals, there must be a planned program for each objective. Programming is like following the proper sequence of a map provided for travel on certain highways to reach a desired destination.

During the Polaris nuclear submarine development, the United States Navy developed a planning system referred to as Project Evaluation Research Technique, often abbreviated to PERT. The development of the Polaris project involved the assimilation of great amounts of information and assigning many tasks. The manager of such a project could have been overwhelmed with the complexity of all the component elements. Thus PERT was developed to assist in the coordination of subsidiary projects and setting them in orderly sequence to lead to the eventual nuclear submarine construction.

The PERT technique can be used in various church-related projects. It begins in a group brainstorming session in which an effort is made to write on a three-by-five card every activity necessary to complete the project.

For instance, if a church is planning a Family Life Conference, the leader would write on cards such component parts as "Speaker Invited," "Speaker Confirmed," "Budget Adopted," "Entertainment Arranged," "Special Music Arranged," "Church Board

Approval Obtained," "Advertising Printed," "Advertising and News Articles Mailed," "Posters Printed," "Posters Displayed," "Newspaper Article Submitted," "Conference Begun," "Conference Completed," "Bills Paid," "Evaluation Made," and "Report to Church Board Completed." Notice that each component is stated in past tense. When the pastor is satisfied he has listed all the component parts of the conference, the three-by-five cards are then taken to a large table or even a floor area, where they are placed in a sequence that will reflect a flow of activity. Usually the first event is placed to the left, with all other items being connected by lines flowing to the right. A sample PERT chart of the suggested "Family Life Conference" appears on the following page. There will be occasions when several components should be completed at the same time, and this will be indicated by such cards being in a straight line vertically (or horizontally if set up that way).

The chart will also show lines indicating a date sequence from the time the planning begins until the project is completed. Once the chart is completed, the pastor can follow the "flow." Thus he is guided in the sequence of events and assures himself that no component has been overlooked which would jeopardize the final outcome. PERT is an important planning tool. Such a chart should be drawn for every major project.

Scheduling

Scheduling as seen in the PERT chart is simply assigning time goals to the various components of planning. When there is a given time of completion, it is then easy to work backwards, in time sequence, to see when the project must be started. Many plans failed

33

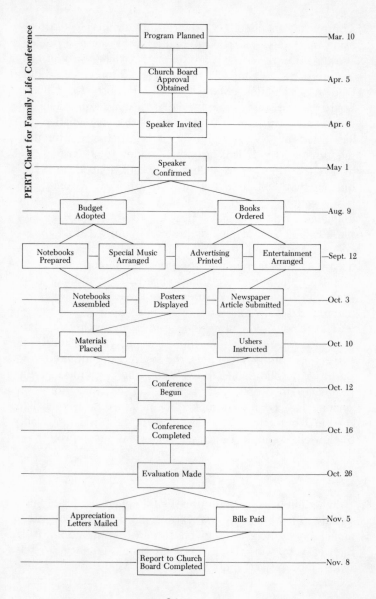

PERT Chart for Family Life Conference

Program Planned — Mar. 10

Church Board Approval Obtained — Apr. 5

Speaker Invited — Apr. 6

Speaker Confirmed — May 1

Budget Adopted / Books Ordered — Aug. 9

Notebooks Prepared / Special Music Arranged / Advertising Printed / Entertainment Arranged — Sept. 12

Notebooks Assembled / Posters Displayed / Newspaper Article Submitted — Oct. 3

Materials Placed / Ushers Instructed — Oct. 10

Conference Begun — Oct. 12

Conference Completed — Oct. 16

Evaluation Made — Oct. 26

Appreciation Letters Mailed / Bills Paid — Nov. 5

Report to Church Board Completed — Nov. 8

34

because they were not started in time. Scheduling will also help the pastor control the flow of work by assuring that the various components are accomplished in the given time frame.

Budgeting

The allocation of resources is indispensable for moving a plan from an idea stage to satisfactory completion. As pointed out, although we normally think of budget as money, budgeting also involves the proper allocation of personnel, materials, and working skills. In order to accomplish a certain task, there should be a budgeting of a certain number of people who have specific skills, and the gathering of tools and facilities necessary for the function. For instance, in planning the "Family Life Conference," there may be needed a major speaker, six ushers, a pianist, an organist, a platform manager, six group discussion leaders, and four special musicians. The leader is budgeting personnel resources when he determines how many people are needed and makes arrangements for their availability. A place to hold the meetings will be needed, and such material resources as overhead projectors, screens, public-address systems, recording equipment, questionnaire cards, musical instruments, songbooks, study books, pencils, and so forth.

A large part of budgeting has to do with finance. True, the church is not a moneymaking business, but it must receive sufficient money to finance God's work. The pastor must clearly and unapologetically present the claims of Christian stewardship to his people. He will need to instruct new people concerning the biblical admonition to give tithes and offerings. A pastor must adequately plan the finances of his church and guide the people in proper stewardship, including the faithful giving of tithes and offerings.

In order to lead the church into an effective ministry, the pastor needs an overall local church budget to guide in the receiving and spending of money. No church is too small for a local annual budget. Occasionally people object to having a church budget on the excuse that they prefer to operate by faith. Such an objection is probably made by a person who has never tried to plan a budget. Few things will challenge your faith more than the annual attempt to develop a realistic budget.

When a pastor arrives at a new church assignment, he should immediately acquaint himself with the previously adopted budget. If he finds no budget, he must then gather as much financial information as he can and establish a budget to give some guidance as to the church's potential income and expenses.

Annual budget planning is a significant part of the pastor's leadership role. A good time to start the new year's budget is in the tenth month of the preceding year. After having recieved the tenth month's financial report, the pastor should have fairly good information to make a projection for the entire year. He will usually develop the preliminary budget for the coming year with the finance committee. The finance committee would then review the budget, make whatever changes they felt were necessary, and submit it to the church board in the twelfth month. It could then be adopted by the board and become the financial guide for the new year.

A sample comprehensive church budget is listed in Appendix D. Its outline is comprehensive enough to serve churches of almost any size, though actual figures will, of course, vary greatly. Small churches may not have budget entries on every line item. Larger churches with more elaborate programs could expand the budget as necessary. The budget form has detailed line items which help to give adequate coverage of all church programs.

Budget forms with too few line items tend to overlook certain expenses, and thus they are inaccurate. In order to give budget control, the budget form must be in sufficient detail to identify every category of expense. The sample form in the appendix is divided into 10 basic categories: local operational fund, building fund and debt reduction, building maintenance, evangelism, special interests, Sunday school, NYI, NWMS, designated funds, and giving to others (denominational budgets). An eleventh category is suggested for special enterprises which the church may sponsor, such as day-care centers. These 11 categories appear both on the receipts and disbursement pages, to provide a plan for a balanced budget.

Planning the Budget

Before the pastor begins serious budget work, he plans the church's ministry for the new year and has an estimate of what the new programs will cost. *(Budgeting always follows purpose.)* First we must know what we want to do and then allocate financial support to the proposals for ministry. In a vital, growing church, the pastor recommends increases for additional church activity, new programs, and rising costs. In budget planning the pastor also considers last year's expenditures as a reasonable beginning estimate for the new year. A very useful device and its instructions for working through all of the ingredients for a viable church budget can be found in Appendix E.

Procedures

A procedure is a predetermined plan which explains the exact chronological steps in attaining some objective. They are sometimes called repetitive use plans. In the Sunday school, for example, the steps involved in selecting a teacher are outlined in the *Manual*. This is a procedure, a type of plan, which guides the church in choosing its instructors. Procedures are mostly used in recurring activities and are useful in helping church workers with routine decisions because they break the process into specific tasks. They are useful to the decision makers because the procedures need not be reviewed each time a decision is needed.

Policies

Policies provide elastic but boundary limits within which a manager can act. Policies help the pastor-manager make decisions within accepted limitations. A church may have a policy to house guest speakers in a motel, but the choice of motels including the price may be left to the judgment of the pastor or a committee chairman. The church may have a policy for an annual insurance review to control costs and to care for inflationary replacement building costs, but the actual month in which such a review is made may be left to the discretion of the church treasurer or the chairman of the board of trustees. Policies allow the leader to make decisions within desirable limits previously decided by the group. Obviously policies must be in keeping with objectives and the statement of purpose.

Chapter 3

LEADERSHIP STRATEGIES FOR DECISION MAKING AND COMMUNICATION

Leading is the implementation phase of management. In this function, the pastor leads his people in decision making, communication, motivation, recruiting, and training. This is the active and highly visible part of church management. This work, which requires close contact with people, is very important to the success of the church.

Preaching and teaching are powerful forms of leadership. In these functions the pastor ties the church to biblical objectives by communicating ideas and motivating the people to action.

Planning, organizing, and controlling are frequently accomplished out of public view. But the pastor must use the ingredients of leadership to secure the attention of his followers and motivate them to effective Christian service. This is the most dynamic management role.

Decision Making

Decision making is frequently the pastor's greatest challenge. Good decisions are not often made easily.

He needs awareness and information for this task. He must pray, search the Scriptures, analyze the problems, evaluate resources, anticipate results, and then boldly take action. There is no way for a pastor to lead without taking the responsibility for decision making which often has far-reaching consequences.

Hesitancy in making decisions frequently hinders achievement. Failure to decide often results in demoralization of the people one leads. Followers cannot long tolerate a leader who refuses to make decisions.

Charles Flory believes that "the biggest thief of time is indecision."[1] And he is right.

In addition to follower frustration, indecision also adversely effects the leader. In *The Time Trap*, Alec MacKensie says:

> Arriving at the point of decisions, many managers vacillate, procrastinate or in other ways refuse to decide. Not only does indecision waste time; it involves worry. It may cause worry, result from it, or simply accompany it, and worry is so destructive that it makes a man tired before he starts his day of work.[2]

MacKensie argues with Flory as to the appropriate time to make decisions. He says, "Fifteen percent of the problems coming to an executive need to mature, five percent shouldn't be answered at all, and the remaining 80 percent should be decided *now*."[3] And those percentages are probably accurate for most pastors.

Fear of making mistakes is the greatest barrier to decision making. Frequently pastors hope that something will happen to make their deciding unnecessary or at least the answer become obvious—a kind of vain hope that all will work out well by delay. But there is solace in the realization that not many leaders always avoided mistakes. Million-dollar mistakes frequently are made by major industries. In spite of such errors prominent managers have been able to throw off the stigma of the bad decision with the realization that even in mistakes they learn something worthwhile.

Thomas Huxley saw growth possibilities in poor decisions. He said:

> Next to being right, the best of all things is to be clearly and definitely wrong, because you will come out somewhere. If you go buzzing about between right and wrong, vibrating and fluctuating, you come out nowhere; but if you are absolutely and thoroughly wrong, you must have the good fortune of knowing the facts that will set you all straight again.[4]

A pastor can be immobilized by the fear of failure. He may not only refuse to make the decision, but lack the courage to delegate it to one of his subordinates because their mistake will reflect on him. Such fear can atrophy an entire church.

All decisions involve risk. Pastors sometimes struggle over decisions because they do not have all the pertinent facts. It is not often that pastors will have all the information they need, or at least think they need, in order to make a fully informed decision. But the issue is largely one of attitude. Peter Drucker, the management consultant, explains, "Too many managers look on a decision as a problem rather than an opportunity. As a result they tend to settle for the solution with the lowest cost even though it promises the lowest gains."[5] The timid are afraid of decisions; the effective see deciding as a challenging part of progress.

The pastor is frequently tempted to say, "I am waiting for John to take action," or "I need more information about this problem," or "I am still thinking about it," or "Problems like this take time to analyze." What may escape the nondeciding pastor is that his procrastination produces a decision by default.

Alec MacKensie gives this counsel in the matter of handling mistakes: "Honest mistakes are tolerated. Venture mistakes, if the results are not disastrous, are applauded. Call your men in, advised Saul Gellerman, and ask them to tell you about the last "good" error they made. If they can't think of one, you have a real problem. No one making no mistakes can be attempting much that is really worthwhile."[6]

Thus in the management work of decision making, there must be some tolerance for mistakes. But the pastor must decide. How are decisions made?

1. DEFINE THE PROBLEM

Basic to decision making is the ability to define the real problem. Leaders are frequently tempted to bypass this hard work of accurately identifying the problem. Problem solving is comparatively easy; identifying the real problem is more difficult. If the analysis is not thorough, the leader may find himself dealing only with symptoms. In making decisions, the leader needs to persevere until he can accurately define the problem.

2. THE PROCESS OF DECISION MAKING

There is a logical process in decision making which often follows these steps:

a. What is the apparent problem? What is the complaint? What seems to be the irritation or failure?

b. What are the facts? In determining this, we must know something about the situation, the kind of people involved, the place of the problem, the timing, and the apparent causative factor.

c. The decision maker will then come to the question *What is the real problem?* After gathering the facts, it may become apparent that the stated problem is not the real problem.

d. When the real problem has been determined, the next step is to *consider possible solutions.* Here the leader may write down the various solutions that come to him. Usually there will be one fairly apparent solution. Further reflection will take him to a second or alternative solution that may be diametrically opposed to the first. The leader must then look for a third solution or perhaps a compromise. The answer is not frequently found in the first or second alternatives. Usually a third, a fourth, fifth, and even more will surface.

e. Anticipate unfavorable reaction. Every action produces change and change always produces resistance. Before setting the apparent solution into action, the leader will consider reactions. He asks, "What will happen when I do this?" The leader must anticipate resistance and make a judgment as to whether the risk is worthwhile. Does the solution positively outweight the negative responses?

The Holy Spirit's guidance in problem solving is always needed, for human abilities are never totally adequate. Then, too, it must be recognized that God may work in ways that are totally surprising. But most often He works through the reasoning abilities He has given to His dedicated people. His ways are most often found in following logical processes.

Before the leader can communicate, or motivate people, it is imperative that he make a decision as to what course of action he will pursue. And some of his most valuable assistance for decision making comes through the combined judgment of Spirit-filled men.

Communication

"The power to communicate is the power to lead"[7] is the way David Sarnoff of RCA said it. It is estimated that 70 percent of the pastor's time may be spent in communication. Once the right course of action has been determined, the leader will then exercise his communication role. A pastor must communicate to succeed as a leader. Many well-intended pastors have failed to achieve their goals simply because they did not satisfactorily communicate their ideas to the congregation.

Communication may be defined as the art of creating understanding. Someone has an idea to communicate to another person. Communication is the complicated art of transmitting that idea from your mind to the mind of another person. The responsibility for securing understanding rests primarily on the person initiating the communication.

In 1 Cor. 14:9, Paul suggests viable communications principles: "Unless you speak intelligible words with your tongue, how will anyone know what you are saying? You will just be speaking into the air" (NIV).

1. COMMUNICATION FLOW

The communication process generally follows four channels: asking, telling, listening, and understanding.

a. Asking. Communication begins by discerning what is in the other person's mind. One need not know a great deal about a person if his communication is simply "Open the window." But if he wants to communicate a technical, theological, or philosophical idea, he will need to know something about the person's basic understanding. Communication frequently breaks

44

down when the leader does not seek an understanding of the listener's background.

Such questions usually fall into three categories. The first, *informational*, deals with facts such as How many? Who? How much? Where? and When? The second is the *ideational* question which is basically subjective. Here the person asks what the other thinks or what he suggests or even how he feels about a certain issue. Thirdly, there is the *evaluational* question. This is a question which asks a man to evaluate his work, his ideas, his concepts, or anything else with which he is associated. If you ask evaluational questions before you ask ideational or informational, you may alienate your listener.

The communicator will ask open questions which allow the other person to freely express what he feels. An example of an open question may be "Tell me, Bob, how this situation looks to you." But a closed question is "Bob, I know you are a committed Christian, and you would not be in favor of this program if you felt it was wrong, would you?" There is only one answer to this last question. Open questions avoid the impression that this is the last word!

The good communicator will ask leading questions rather than loaded ones. A leading question will give general directions to the reply but are not restrictive to any one answer. An example of a leading question is "Bob, this is a difficult situation. How would you go about working out a solution?" A loaded question immediately puts the other man on the defensive, such as "Bob, I know this is a difficult situation, but what makes you think you have the right solution?" Here the man approached will have to justify his actions first before he can analyze the solution. This is not the climate in which good communication can occur.

Finally, the communicator should ask cool rather than heated questions. The cool question will avoid as much emotion as possible and deal primarily with appeals to reason. An example of a cool question is "Bob, in coming to a solution to this difficult situation, what would you recommend to be the first steps to a satisfactory agreement?" The heated question would be something like "Bob, let's cut out the foolishness because we have been around and around on this matter. Just tell me what you think we should do." The heated question stirs emotion that will often stand in the way of logical thinking.

b. Telling. The art of articulation is the transfering of a message you want to deliver into understandable words. There are four steps to telling or sharing information.

(1) The communicator must first of all get an audience. He must attract the attention of the people to whom he wants to deliver a message. Often these people are not ready to receive a message. They may be tired, emotionally upset, or preoccupied with other concerns. The communicator must do or say something to make them aware of the fact that he has a message to deliver.

(2) The communicator must build a bridge to his audience. This is an attempt to move from where you are to whatever the interest of the other party may be. Preaching, which is the pastor's most common form of communication, must be relevant and designed to meet the real needs of his people. The pastor needs to understand his people and be alert to their interests. Preaching should not follow only the personal study interests of the pastor but rather be directed to the needs of the congregation. There is no communication

46

When we are answering questions nobody is asking. The communicator must relate to the interests of others—build a bridge as it were.

(3) The communicator must illustrate his truth. Illustrations are windows into otherwise concealed truth. The best illustrations come from human life situations in which the listeners can easily identify themselves. They should be realistic and contemporary.

(4) Finally, the communicator calls for action. The purpose of the sermon should be the impelling of people to take certain courses of action. After the communicator has received the attention of the audience, built a bridge to their interests, and illustrated the truth, he can then make his appeal for action.

c. *Listening.* The effective communicator will be a person who can be reached by others. He listens. He is obviously trying to understand his people. Frequently our communication is defective because we have not taken the time to listen to others. Preachers often make poor listeners because they spend so much of their time talking. But real listening is both a learnable and useful skill.

d. *Understanding.* We must realize that communication is not necessarily agreement but rather understanding. Many of our church problems are the results of misunderstanding rather than disagreement. In our hurry to do many things, we frequently do not take the time to try to understand people. Remember, the hearer attaches a meaning to our statements. The effective communicator is concerned that his hearers attach the right kind of meaning to what he says.

Communication failures are caused by a number of

47

factors. Sometimes we mistake the medium of communication for the process itself. We may mistakenly believe that communication has occurred simply because we have preached a sermon. Sometimes the emotions of our listeners block communication. The parishioner who had an automobile accident on the way to church, and fears the possibility of court action, may not be in any attitude to accurately receive our communication. Another person may be suffering from some illness and is preoccupied with his distress. He may not understand what the pastor is saying. Still others are preoccupied with grief or even the anticipation of some pleasant experience and may be completely tuned out. People also tend to hear what they want to hear and can filter out the undesirable. For such people the sermon may not result in effective communication.

Communication comes both formally and informally. Formal communication has to do with words, letters, memoranda, books, and sermons. Informal communication has to do with body language such as facial expressions, posture, and actions.

The good communicator understands that words are tools. Words represent ideas. They are not things in themselves, they are symbols. For example, it has been discovered that the word *round* has 70 distinctly different meanings. Words with multiple meanings can be understood only in context. Words must be chosen to convey the right ideas. Words, given a different definition, may also tend to obscure meaning. In the English language many words have numerous definitions and can be understood only in context. So words have meaning given to them by both the speaker and the listener.

2. Improving Your Communication

The leader must definitely know what he wants to say. He should have thought through his message. His purpose should be well in mind, and he should know what he wants to communicate.

The communicator should understand his audience. The pastor should know the people among whom he works and the situations in which they live. Ideally, the longer the pastor serves the church, the better he knows his people and the more effective will be his communication.

The leader must strive to get understanding from his followers. This begins by starting with issues that have mutual agreement. He should use simple, concrete words. Communication is more effective by the use of words of force, such as *freezing, boiling, besieged, breathless*. He should discover and use words of energy to convey his message. Action words are important. The communicator will seek to develop an effective vocabulary. He will also seek to eliminate unnecessary words. Many preachers have problems in being too wordy. The punch line of an illustration might be dissipated by too many details given in the story. Excessive verbiage not only obscures the message but tires the people. The communicator should protect his primary message by not allowing too much secondary information to overshadow the main thrust of the communication.

The communicator must make good use of feedback. Feedback to a speaker consists of the facial expressions of the people, their reactions to his statements, and their general attention to what he has to say. The communicator will interpret what he sees and hears and use the evaluation to strengthen what he says next.

The following 10 rules for good communication are adapted from the American Management Association.

a. Seek to clarify the ideas you wish to communicate.

b. Examine the true purpose of each communication.

c. Consider the total physical and human setting whenever you communicate.

d. Consult with others, where appropriate, in planning communications.

e. Be mindful, while you communicate, of the overtones as well as the basic content of your message.

f. Take the opportunity, when it arrives, to convey something of help or value to the receiver.

g. Follow up your communications.

h. Communicate for tomorrow as well as today.

i. Be sure your actions support your communications.

j. Last, but by no means least, seek not only to be understood but to understand—be a good listener.[8]

Communication in pastoral management is the attempt by the leader to make decisions known to the largest number of persons in the church constituency. Here for his followers the leader makes sense of the ideas, facts, and happenings with which he has wrestled. No decision will provide achievement unless it captures the imagination and commitment of the people who carry it out. Their wholehearted acceptance finally determines the success of his management leadership.

Chapter 4

LEADERSHIP STRATEGIES ON THE HUMAN SIDE

People are the church's main reason for existence. Human relationships determine the quality of ministry and sometimes set a ceiling on growth in a local church. Most pastoral managers are both fascinated and frustrated by the unpredictability of people. Understanding and working with the human element provides the most urgent challenge faced by contemporary pastors.

The pastor must inspire confidence, enlist courage, and win support by making people want to get wholeheartedly behind a plan. All of this and much more forms the human side of church management.

Motivation

The effective pastor must move people to action. Followers must be motivated so acceptance and action result from their own decisions. A number of men have failed in their pastoral ministries because they were unable to motivate people to inspired service. Effective motivation of people involves meeting a need which they feel and provides one or more satisfiers of that need.

Motivation increases when the task is sufficiently challenging to capture the imagination and energy of the participants. This is accomplished by high motivating factors like spiritual growth, recognition, responsibility, and achievement. Then, too, the task must be as free as possible from demotivating factors like poor supervision, inadequate policies, low budget, little status, and no appreciation.

Motivation multiplies as the leader involves followers in his management process. J. B. Phillips explains, "When I tell a man what to do, he is a slave; when I explain the reason for its doing, I have increased his stature; when I let him plan with me, I have made him a partner. Motivation will follow proportionately these actions."[1] This shared leadership attitude is basic to motivating followers.

The classic Herzberg Study shows 10 major factors which motivate persons to action: (1) achievement, (2) recognition, (3) work itself, (4) responsibility, (5) advancement, (6) organization policy, (7) competence and fairness of leaders, (8) interpersonal relations, (9) salary, and (10) working conditions.[2] Contrary to what many believe, salary and working conditions are the least important factors in occupational motivation. Achievement and the accomplishment of some worthy goal were first on the list. Although the study was made on the basis of secular employment, the parallel can be drawn to the church.

Maslow's laws are well known to students of psychology. In *Motivation and Personality*, A. H. Maslow states man's five basic needs:

1. Physiological (hunger, appetite)
2. Security
3. Belongingness or love
4. Self-esteem
5. Self-actualization[3]

These concepts can be visualized in the form of a triangle with various layers beginning with primary needs at the bottom and moving to the most sophisticated level of self-actualization.

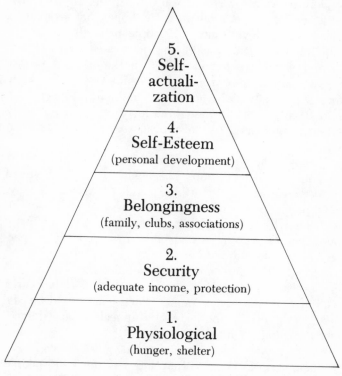

Maslow's Chart of Man's Basic Needs

People can be motivated to service by helping them to see that their needs can be met in the order of the triangle, beginning at the bottom and working towards the top. If people are hungry, they can be motivated to do certain things by the hope of getting food—motivation at the most elemental level. People who have these basic needs met may feel insecure about the future. This group of people can be moved to action by giving them the hope that they will have security and protection from harm.

Persons whose first two levels of needs are fairly well met may be motivated by hopes of acceptance, belonging, or love. Since all people need to be accepted, followers can usually be motivated by offering them belongingness. Still higher in the triangle is motivation that comes from self-esteem. This is the hope that a person will better understand and respect himself. People with the first three levels of need met may often be motivated by an appeal to the fourth level of self-esteem.

Finally, people may be motivated on the highest level of self-actualization. This involves the inner need to be creative, to contribute, and to grow. Usually, only people with the first four levels of need can be motivated by this appeal to a ministry. A study made by "Men in Action" reveals that perhaps only 3 percent of people respond here.

The pastor must know his people and understand the levels on which they can be motivated. If he works with people who have unmet shelter and food needs, they can hardly be motivated by appeals to acceptance. On the other hand, people who live on the higher planes of needs cannot be challenged by lesser levels.

Then, too, a leader often fails to motivate people because his message is really directed to meet his own needs. His message may ultimately be meant to give him acceptance with people.

Another leader may fail when his approach to his followers is as though they all had the same need. Obviously the motivation of a large group of people becomes more complex because different people have varying needs. Thus group motivation is usually very limited and of short duration. The fact is, motivation is best accomplished by an individualistic approach where the leader tries to motivate each follower according to his personal need level. This makes it all the more important that the pastor know his parishioners on an individual basis.

Ten motivational guidelines have been listed in a study made my "Men in Action."

1. Human beings are always motivated at some level and in some direction.

2. Motivation always involves some goal.

3. Most motives are learned, not inherited.

4. Human desires precede motivations.

5. Motivation is most effective in behavior when a man has a clear concept of his goals.

7. Motivation is inseparable from one's values, needs, and desires.

8. Information regarding the goal's distance is a powerful motivator.

9. The terms of one's motivation are defined by the individual.

10. One's self-image is powerfully related both to the direction and the limits of his motivation.

In 1957, Prof. Douglas McGregor of Massachusetts Institute of Technology advanced the so-called Theory X and Theory Y concepts of motivation. Theory X assumptions about people are:

1. Human beings are inherently lazy and will shun work if they can.

2. People must be directed, controlled, and motivated by fear of punishment or deprivation to impel them to work as the company requires.

3. The average human being prefers to be directed, wishes to avoid responsibility, has relatively little ambition, and wants security above all.

Theory Y assumptions about people are:

1. For most people the expenditure of physical and mental effort in work is as natural as for play or rest.

2. Man will exercise self-control in the service of objectives which he accepts.

3. Under proper conditions the average human being learns not only to accept responsibility but also to seek it.

4. The capacity for exercising imagination, ingenuity, and creativity exists generally among people.[4]

Probably neither of these assumptions is altogether true. However, leaders generally tend to accept one or the other of these concepts about the people they lead. If a leader assumes Theory X, he will try to motivate people by force or threat. If he is a Theory Y leader, he will tend to motivate people by encouraging them to reach their goals and be creative. The pastor being aware of these assumptions can work in harmony with them. The pastor who tries to motivate people under Theory X sees his people living below the Spirit-filled life and/or immature. Hopefully, the pastor working with church members should be able to motivate people from Theory Y assumptions.

While secular management provides profound insights into human motivation, it must be frankly affirmed that the church has vast additional motivation resources. Those assets are found in the basic instruction of Jesus to Peter, "Feed my sheep" (John 21:17). Like one thoughtful layman said, "If we had been providing more spiritual feeding experiences where people could get what they are after out of church, the sanctuary would be full for every service."

The Pastor as Change Agent

Is change good or bad? The issue may be hotly debated. Of course, we must understand the purpose of change before we can make a judgment. Different does not always mean better.

Conservative people value preserving the past and reducing change. Progressive people are more inclined to innovation and search for improvement. Leadership can be both conservative and progressive. When it comes to biblical authority and sound doctrine, we resist change. At the same time, we may be open to change when we think in terms of new methods to meet contemporary conditions.

Since there is always uncertainty about the future, change generally produces fear. Often a leader feels he has insufficient information to cause change. And some people are simply satisfied with the past or with what they have, so they have little interest in change. Action-oriented people are usually more concerned with immediate details than with long-range objectives, consequently they may sometimes resist change.

The pastor needs always to consider the possible positive result of change. Most present-day programs were at their inception innovations. Everything we do was once a change from an established procedure. While not all change is improvement, there is no improvement without change. Only the perfect needs no change. The pastor must be stimulated by a vision of better things. He must be able to share his dream. Every great Christian leader first saw possible improvement and then led his people into change which produced positive results.

Jesus explained the inability of old "wineskins" to hold "new wine." "Wineskins" refers to form while "wine" refers to content. New power, new discovery, new stimulation, new achievement is seldom contained in old forms. The Holy Spirit is dynamic; Pentecost was a time of great change. Throughout church history, revival and significant renewal have produced results but were always accompanied by painful change.

The pastor as agent of change ministers midway between where people are and where they ought to be. Because he sees farther than his followers, he must be the change instrument. Since change produces problems, the church needs leaders to manage these adjustments. The pastoral manager leads his church past their dreams to the fulfillment of their potential. This is done by helping followers see the advantages of the proposed change.

Where would the church and society be without innovators? Paul was an innovator when he began preaching the gospel in Gentile countries. That had not been done before. Many people, even good people, misunderstood his motive. Resistance to change often keeps the innovator from being a popular person. But the innovator is not content to be inhibited by possible misunderstanding. He weighs personal risks in order to produce improvements for the kingdom of God and rests in the confidence that the consequential effects will be worth the effort.

Methods and message are not the same. As stated at the outset, worship, evangelism, discipleship, fellowship, and mercy are the great unchanging purposes of the Church. But the methods to accomplish these purposes must be subject to improvement and change. A certain way of doing things is not sacrosanct. Whatever works, as long as it is not in violation of biblical instructions, is legitimate if it truly accomplishes the church's purpose.

There is a fear that innovation will erode the message of the church, but the opposite is true. *If methods remain constant, the message will eventually change!* If a method continues after conditions change, the effect of the message is lost. Leaders, then, are pressured to accommodate to the new, unfavorable conditions, and the impact of their ministry is forfeited. The answer to the message-method controversy is a burning heart set on achieving great Christian goals. Ways must be found to make it through changing conditions by injecting new methods for communicating the changeless message.

In trying to effect change, the pastor should watch for opinion setters. Even though they may not be elected officers or church board members, they are respected people to whom others give attention. Indecisive people are often deeply influenced by the opinion setters in the local church. Thus without manipulation, the pastor must lead the opinion setters to understand and hopefully to agree with his proposals. Then they will lead the way in formulating group opinions, and the change process is under way.

The pastor must be a positive agent of change if he is to lead his people in effective Kingdom service.

Recruitment and Training

Paul's instructions to young Timothy included: "The

things that thou hast heard of me among many witnesses, the same commit thou to faithful men, who shall be able to teach others also" (2 Tim. 2:2). Paul's message is still true for present-day pastors. The only way to multiply God's work is through recruiting and training fellow believers.

The effective manager seeks to develop his skill in making assignments to people. The goal is to place them where their God-given talents can best be used. Recruitment may be defined as getting the right person and the right assignment together. Training is the hard work of helping individuals improve their attitudes, knowledge, and skills.

The Great Commission (Matt. 28:19-20) spells out our task. It is so expansive that we could be overwhelmed by its demand. The Church is to "make disciples of all nations," and that obviously involves the recruiting and training of more Christian workers. The larger a church becomes, the more recruitment and training there is to do. It has been estimated that 80 percent of the church's work is done by 20 percent of the people. If this is true, the greatest part of the unfinished task of recruitment and training is yet to be done.

In recruiting people, the pastor will look for persons who have demonstrated their leadership. However, he must look for potential "diamonds in the rough" that have previously been overlooked. Some persons with great potential can grow into outstanding leaders when given the right opportunities. Such people will always be grateful to the pastor who discovered them, believed in them, and gave them an opportunity to serve.

The personal interview provides a valuable tool for recruitment. If a potential leader is stopped in the church foyer and there urged to accept an assignment, he is likely to consider the task as not worthy of his best effort. However, if the pastor makes a special appointment to see him, at the prospect's convenience, the person will feel that the pastor has something important to discuss.

Is imperative that the recruiter be excited about what he is doing. With credibility, he must magnify the office and help the person being recruited to see the importance of the task.

The recruiter must describe the job in detail. A job description which outlines the duties and responsibilities is a useful tool. The person being recruited does not want to learn later about unexplained details. To the best of his ability, the leader should describe exactly what needs to be done. He should level with his man. (Sample job descriptions can be found in Appendix B.)

Many people are reluctant to serve because they feel inadequate. Thus the recruiter will need to build the person's confidence and assure him that he really can do the task.

Finally, the recruiter must get a decision by setting a deadline for action. This will help the prospective worker not to delay. Let the prospective worker first say yes or no to God, and then ask him to come and tell his decision. If the answer is negative, the pastor should accept it as of the Lord. Such an attitude will leave the door open to ask this person to accept another assignment at a later time.

The matter of training a recruit for a specific task will involve five areas of instruction.

1. *Explain what needs to be done.* This can be accomplished by verbally outlining the duties and supporting this with a written job description. For instance, if you are recruiting a Sunday school teacher,

first tell the person what a teacher does. An instructional book on Sunday school teaching can also be used.

2. *Demonstrate how the work is to be done.* For example, ask the prospective worker to sit in on a class where a competent Sunday school teacher serves. Ask that person to observe the experienced teacher's work for a period of three Sundays.

3. Next ask the prospective worker to *try the job under controlled conditions.* You would then allow the prospective teacher to actually teach the class. Offer to be present in the class or to be available for help should the new teacher need assistance.

4. Now let the recruit *do the job on his own.* In the case of the teacher, let the teacher lead the class for the next four weeks with the understanding that you will not be present. Let the teacher feel the challenge and burden of the class himself.

5. *Follow up the recruit to see how he is getting along.* Ask the new worker how things have gone since he is doing it by himself. Give him the assistance that is necessary, and then encourage him to go on with his new assignment. Ask him to contact you whenever help is needed. Follow-up requires some system of regular meeting with the worker to determine his progress. The good leader will ask for reports from his people. He will provide them with the necessary report forms. With these reports, the leader is able to make periodic evaluations of the worker with the goal of helping him to do a better job.

Leadership Tensions

The leader faces a number of tension sources. Frequently he is tempted to underestimate himself—have a defeatist attitude concerning his own abilities.

On the next page is a chart on which one may rate his leadership capabilities. The idea is to put an X in the column that he believes best fits his characteristics, then repeat the test in a few months. This will reveal if there has been any improvement in leadership skills.

No person can be a leader if he does not trust his followers. Every pastor has been betrayed or at least disappointed, but the effective leader expresses a basic trust in his people. When he does, it is easier for them to trust him.

Distrust of his own judgment may add to a leader's tensions. A pastor-manager must made decisions, and he can be intimidated by the situation in which he fails to trust his own judgment. There needs to be a great deal of prayer, continued reading, developing awareness, and a willingness to check his judgments against the ideas of Spirit-filled followers.

The Test of the Church Manager

The role of leader does not come automatically with the acceptance of a call by a pastor to a particular church. Rather it must be earned. The "proof of the pudding" is one's ability to induce followers to work together with enthusiasm and purpose for the accomplishment of the church's fivefold task of worship, evangelism, discipleship, fellowship, and mercy. The pastor really leads when he helps a church make its plan a reality. This happens when he clearly outlines the tasks of each member in relationship to the church's purpose and generates enthusiasm for the accomplishment of this task.

In short, the effective pastoral leader represents a worthy cause, attracts followers, and inspires their efforts as group members to worthy achievement.

Leadership Evaluation Chart

	VERY	QUITE	SLIGHT	SLIGHT	QUITE	VERY	
Competent							Incompetent
Warm							Cold
Leader							Follower
Positive							Negative
Sincere							Insincere
Listens to Others							Ignores Others
Friendly							Unfriendly
Acts Promptly							Procrastinates
Objective							Emotional
Helps Others							Self-centered
Fair							Unfair
Solves Problems							Ignores Problems
Permits Initiative							Restricts Initiative
Sees Both Sides							Sees One Side Only
Approachable							Aloof
Satisfied							Frustrated
Bright							Dull
Speaks Up							Silent
Flexible							Stubborn
Sees Overall Picture							Sees Petty Details
Relaxed							Tense
Open-minded							Close-minded
Gets to Point							Indirect

Chapter 5

ORGANIZING FOR ACHIEVEMENT

"Let's get organized." "This church needs more organization." "We need less organization." The word *organize* is heard frequently in churches everywhere. Sometimes these statements are smoke screens to hide mediocre work, but most often they represent a felt need for organization improvement.

General Foods Corporation defines organization as a plan by which a group of people pool their efforts toward designated objectives through definition and division of activities, responsibilities and authority. Why do we give a man this job and give him this authority and allow him to make these kinds of decisions? Because together that is the best way to accomplish the goal.[1]

Organization implies a relationship between purpose, people, and work tasks. Organization may be understood as identifying jobs to be done and relating people to the effective accomplishment of tasks. Thus organization is an important part of management because it puts people and work together to achieve desired results.

Open to Change

Olan Hendrix, in his book *Management and the Christian Worker,* relates the following story: In a recent issue of *U.S. News and World Report,* there was an interesting story about a British military team trying to cut down on the manpower used in handling a field cannon. Always there had been six men assigned to each cannon, but there were only five jobs. The men studied each job and went to the instruction manual. From the first edition on, every manual called for a crew of six. Finally they located the man who had written the manual originally, a retired general, and they asked him what the sixth man was supposed to do. He replied, "The sixth man? He holds the horses." They had not used horses for many, many years, but the job persisted. No reason was necessary; precedent was reason enough![2]

Churches can be like that!

Institutionalism, a dread disease of the church, tends to flourish when our ministries operate solely on tradition rather than current need. Many church organizations have changed very little over the years even though the church seeks to do its work with people who have experienced as much change in one decade as used to take a century. For this generation the effective, serving church must be flexible in its organization and responsive to the Lord as He leads into new ministries. The organization to support such ministries must be dynamic and always open to improvement.

Church purpose provides the basic foundation for all upgrading of organization. Organizational structure should be suggested by the pastor and adopted by the church board. The organizational chart must be flexible to allow for changing conditions, new goals, and chart is to help structure people's work relationship and to make them understood. The probability of reaching our goals increases when personnel, tasks, and objectives are related in ways which are clearly understood by all who are involved.

Organization for What?

A statement from "Men in Action" says:

Of course the church does not exist for itself, that is, for the beauty of its organization, the symmetry of its parts, the majesty of its services; it exists for its product and for the truth which has been committed to it and of which it is the support and stay in the world. But just on that account, not less but more, is it necessary that it be properly organized and administered— that it may function properly. Beware how you tamper with any machine, lest you mar it or its product; beware how you tamper with or are indifferent to the Divine organization and ordering of the church, lest you thereby mar its efficiency or destroy its power, as the pillar and ground of the truth. Surely you can trust God to know it is best to organize His church so that it may perform its function in the world.[3]

The purpose of organization is summarized by Alvin Brown in these words: "Organization defines the part which each member of an enterprise is expected to perform and the relationships between such members to the end that their concerted effort or endeavors shall be most effective for the purpose of the enterprise."[4]

Some churches and their pastors resist the idea of formal structure and stated organization. Perhaps they have had experiences where a static organization strangled church life. Organizational rigidity always cripples a church, but dynamic organization which is well understood by the members of a church greatly increases its possibilities of growth.

People-centered Organization

Are organizations made for people or people made for organizations? True, institutions, especially the church, need to prosper, but that is best done with a clear-cut emphasis on the importance of people. Church organizations must be shaped to serve people. For instance, there were no lay leaders in the Early Church until a person-centered need arose (Acts 6). The tendency is to approach each new situation with a preconceived organizational structure rather than to approach the need with stated purposes and then develop an organizational structure to achieve those goals.

Organizations need frequent renewal or they become self-centered, obese, clumsy, or even oppresive. The greatest way to achieve organizational renewal is to have an effective program to develop new talent and incorporate new people. Spiritually gifted people with new vision must be frequently fed into the organization to keep it effectively alive.

Organizations should not be controlled by any one person or by any group of people. Vested interests must not be allowed to determine the church's ministry.

The organization must not allow its workers to feel like cogs in a machine. The healthy organization has an atmosphere in which people can express their ideas. Their involvement in the organizational processes should help them grow as Christians. All of this can happen as they share their efforts to achieve worthy, well-defined goals.

The church is people—People working, people witnessing, people caring, people winning. The organization must be large enough to include everyone in its mission. People participate when they are involved in meaningful tasks.

Future Focus

All organizations, and especially the church, must be more concerned about what it is becoming than what it has been. The leader of the organization must be more conscious of the "windshield" than the "rearview mirror." The organization, while resisting the temptation to act only in accordance with its past, must be alert to present opportunities. It needs realistic ideas of how it can positively shape its future.

The best organizational procedure functions only as a vehicle of goal achievement. New developments in the community, church, and people's lives call for constant organizational evaluation.

Appendix A suggests a sample local church organizational chart. Each church will need a different structure; it is important that each church develop such an organizational chart to provide an overview of its work. A significant reason for all organization structure is to provide a well-defined purpose for all group members.

Delegation

In the eighteenth chapter of Exodus, we have one of the first biblical illustrations of delegation. Moses carried great responsibility for his people; in fact, he was worn down by his heavy duties. Jethro, Moses' father-in-law, observed what was happening and knew that in such an exhausted condition Moses was not able to make sound judgments. Thus the people ultimately would suffer from lack of good leadership. Jethro proposed that Moses share his work with capable men. Moses recruited other leaders and delegated authority. Thus Moses' burden was lightened, and he had greater personal resources to make good judgments. Now the people received efficient, prompt leadership.

This scriptural incident speaks to pastors. To effectively lead a church, pastors must share responsibility. And as churches grow, the importance of delegating authority increases.

Delegation is necessary for organization health. When it is properly executed, it can become the means of greater development for existing leaders plus the discovery of new leaders.

Delegation has three basic parts. The first is *responsibility*. This implies a task, a duty, a ministry to perform. The pastor-manager will delegate responsibility for certain ministries to his people. *Authority* is the second term. The person being held responsible for a certain function should have the authority to do this task. He must be given authority to make decisions at his level. The third term is *accountability*. This implies reporting. The person to whom responsibility has been given must be accountable and report to his superior on the progress of his assignment.

Organizational structures assume that a leader have only as many subordinates as he can effectively oversee. Generally in the secular management field this is a one-to-seven ratio. However, in volunteer organizations including the church, this number may be larger and is determined by the amount of work expected of subordinates. So, when people have only a few things to do, the manager may be able to oversee more than the recommended maximum of seven persons.

But when is delegation needed in the local church? Obviously when deadlines are often missed. Also when a new challenge is conceived, the leader delegates more of the routine functions so he can more deeply involve himself in this latest project. The pastor needs to delegate when he finds himself doing trivial tasks that others could do. Again, the constant reoccurrence of crises usually indicates that too few persons are attempting too much. Delegation will also lower stress conflict. The wise pastor should not be overworked but should delegate before this condition develops.

Admittedly, delegation is not easy for some leaders. Often they feel God has called them to certain ministries, and thus it is not acceptable for them to delegate these tasks to others. Neither will the pastor delegate if he expects complete uniformity. Weak leaders frequently fear competition and thus are threatened when someone else does too much too well. Tradition or the desire for prestige and control also keeps a leader from delegating. Some pastors are not willing to pay the price in time and effort to train others and hence struggle along carrying the whole load themselves. They will never have potential leaders to whom they can delegate if they do not train them.

Job Descriptions

Job descriptions are important for effective organization. They sould include the church *Manual's* description of assignment. However, the *Manual* does not endeavor to anticipate every local situation; it simply provides basic guidance. So a more detailed expansion will be needed.

The pastor is the logical person to initiate the job descriptions, since he has a comprehensive view of the church and theoretically knows how to do all required jobs. From this firsthand knowledge, job descriptions can be developed. A conference with persons presently functioning in these tasks also helps determine what the job requires and how this work is presently being done. He should then present the job descriptions to the church board for adoption and inclusion in the church's policy book, *Standard Practices*. One by one, job descriptions can be presented to the church board for adoption.

Whenever a new officer is elected, the job description is taken from the *Standard Practice* notebook and photocopied. The original is put back into the notebook for future reference and the photocopy given to the new worker. Workers need encouragement to continually analyze work and make recommendations for updating their job descriptions. Thus job descriptions are kept dynamic, and none are allowed to bind workers to outmoded functions. Appendix B shows a sample job description.

Every worker who is assigned to some task has a right to know what is expected of him in his assignment. The mere provision of such a document causes all persons—church board, pastor, and prospective workers—to view each service assignment as having a significant importance.

Pastor and Board Relationships

Effective churches usually have wholesome relationships between church board and pastor. Ideally the church board and pastor recognize their respective functions and work together harmoniously.

Since the *Manual* provides that the pastor is chairman of the board, careful attention should be given to the chairman's function. At the outset of a new pastorate, both pastor and board should fully understand their areas of responsibility. The church board should deal with the matter of overall church policy but not attempt to dictate the pastoral functions such as preaching and pastoral care. Neither should the pastor assume responsibilities that belong to the church board.

As chairman of the board, the pastor is responsible for seeing that the board's directives are followed. The pastor should protect himself from overwork by making sure that the implementation of board decisions are assigned at the board meeting to capable lay persons.

Basic to good interpersonal relationships should be the pastor's recognition that the church board is a body of duly elected representatives who have mutual interests. They decide all policy matters. The church board and pastor relationships should never be allowed to disintegrate so either views the other as an obstacle to progress.

The pastor should endeavor to keep the board informed on all matters pertaining to the church's ministry. He should be open and frank—sharing both victories and problems. He should encourage their suggestions for improvements. As chairman, he is responsible for helping the board move the church to the fulfillment of its goals.

The pastor also serves as a resource person to the church board. His training, meaningful day-by-day involvement in people's lives, plus his church management experiences provide him with a valuable reservoir of helpful information. He should not expect the church board to make decisions unless he supplies them with information; they need factual data. The pastor should prepare an agenda for every church board meeting. A sample can be found in Appendix C.

Church boards look to the pastor for suggestions and alternatives. The board then adopts one of the alternatives or even provides other solutions. Reliable action plans are usually developed from a review of purpose, discussion of priorities, thinking beyond the obvious, and exploring all possibilities.

It is important that the pastor-church board relationship function at highly cooperative level. Mutual respect in a setting of genuine Christian commitment significantly contributes to the church's ongoing effectiveness.

When Reorganization Is Needed

As the church increases its effectiveness, the organizational demands grow. So organizing and reorganizing is never complete. Thus the pastor-manager has the continuous challenge of organizing his church for maximum achievement. He builds on two creative tensions: (1) Progress always requires change on someone's part; and (2) The mission and message of the church is changeless. Worthwhile organizational structure makes teamwork possible so that each worker knows his assignment, makes needed decisions, and fulfills his responsibilities effectively. At the same time, he has an understanding of how his activities relate to the whole ministry of the church.

74

Chapter 6

CONTROL—
EVALUATION AND REMEDY

While the management process begins with planning, it continues with purposeful activities which produce come kind of results. These achievements must be evaluated before new planning can begin. Factual data will reveal the true present status of the church. Then the manager is ready to lead his group into either more ambitious achievement or to the correction of existing inadequacies. But where does he get the information needed for evaluation, new planning, and/or correction?

The term *control* may be misunderstood as an effort to manipulate a church. However, management control is not domination of the part of one person over others. Rather, it is a practical help to the pastor in his work of keeping the church progressing towards its goal achievement.

Why Control?

Television coverage of the satellite launchings impressed us with the tremendous technology needed to send such vehicles into outer space. However, after the launch thrust, there must be supporting equipment to control and track the satellite during flight. Elaborate electronic devices, technicians, and tracking stations provide information to measure progress against the expected performance at any given point in the flight. If there is evidence that the satellite is not performing correctly, the technicians are then able to activate mechanisms to correct the missile's flight. Just as important as the powerful launch is the necessary mid-course correction.

The pastor as controller is like this tracking equipment. The goals have been set and the program has been launched; now the pastor must receive continuing information as to the church's performance in comparison to expectations. Such information must be evaluated to enable the pastor to set corrective measures in motion.

In capsule form, control means management effort which determines our status in relationship to our goals, and when necessary it sets remedial action in motion. The pastor who is faithful in his control ministry will constantly need to consider the question "Is my church effective?"

The total church program, and every project within it, needs frequent evaluation. For instance, the pastor may turn his attention to the Sunday school. He needs to study it thoroughly, consider its goals, and then determine whether or not the present Sunday school efforts are really effective in the ministry of teaching and discipleship. Similarly the pastor ought to frequently review his evangelism program with the intent of determining how effective it is in reaching and winning new people to Christ. What about that Sunday morning service? Do the people worship? How about the building program?

Aim of Control

Robert K. Bower lists some functions of controlling:[1]

1. To see that all activities are subservient to the objectives of the organization. There must be interdependence between the different departments in a church.

2. To be a diagnostic aid. Action can thus be taken before serious consequences have resulted from inefficient or irresponsible operations. Though we learn from mistakes, we should also try to avoid them!

3. To provide important data for the formation of future plans.

4. To improve the program. Prompt action can also be taken if good records are kept.

5. To communicate what is being done to interested parties. Church members and outsiders want to know what is going on.

Control Is Scriptural

Control is evident in the Bible. Jesus was concerned with control. In Luke 9:1-10, we have the account of Jesus sending out His disciples and His request that they report to Him. In Luke 10:17, the Lord sends out the 70 elders, and they, too, were to report to Him. In the parables of the unjust steward (Luke 16:1-9) and of the pounds (Luke 19:12-26), Jesus illustrates reporting, accountability, and control. Furthermore, we find that Paul reported to the Christians at Antioch (Acts 14:26-27) and later to the elders at Jerusalem (Acts 15:3-4). These are all biblical forms of control and suggest their importance for the church of today. The pastor must recognize that he is accountable to God, not only for himself but for those whom he leads. Control is a part of God's intention for the church.

Control and Objectives

Obviously, there can be no control unless the purpose has been clearly stated and goals have been set. Progress cannot be evaluated unless there is a fixed statement of purpose.

Pastors and church leaders are involved in a never-ending pursuit for excellence. But this is possible only when they honestly evaluate what they are doing. Remember, only that which is perfect does not need to be changed. Whether the church controls change or change controls it depends largely on whether it will honestly and thoroughly evaluate its programs. In the work of control, consideration is given to the difference between what is and what ought to be. For example, officer and committee reports are given each month to a church board meeting, and the pastor with effective control seriously evaluates these reports. What are the developing trends? Are goals being reached? Is the program on schedule?

The evaluation of the church's ministry falls into two types. First is the *summative*, which is an evaluation of the total end results. This kind of evaluation helps determine the worth of a program. The second type is *formative*, which is an evaluation of the program in process. Here the primary concern is the effectiveness of procedures.

The American Management Association suggests several guidelines for setting performance standards.[2]

1. Jointly developed by superior and worker
2. Statement drafted of basic results expected (This includes the defining of all important duties, responsibilities, and functions in the specified area.)
3. Identification of accurate means of measurement
4. Clear statement to avoid misunderstanding
5. Measurement of both quality and quantity of work performed
6. Attainability
7. Provision for periodic division

To properly evaluate the church's program, the pastor-controller needs a standard of performance built on the statement of purpose. This should include his vision as to what the ideal church should be. What specifically will happen if this church is successful this year? If there is a genuine revival, how will the people know that it has come? Too frequently both the planning and the evaluation are so vague that there is nothing definite by which to measure effectiveness. Obviously, then, the earlier work of establishing definite goals and objectives influences the controlling stage of church management.

Since much of the church's product is of a spiritual nature, it is more difficult to measure on a quantitative report. The spiritual depth of people and their growth in devotion to Christ is not easy to put into numbers. However, it is reasonable to believe that vibrant spiritual life will finally produce statistical growth. Most of the reporting in the church has to do with statistics. This need not be abandoned, but additional ways are needed to evaluate the church's progress.

The Danger of Overcontrol

Workers must be encouraged to innovate. They are more likely to be effective when they are assured of the confidence of their superiors. Frequently they discover better methods, and they should be encouraged to propose them. There is overcontrol when workers feel they are under constant surveillance. This kills the spirit of creativity which needs to be encouraged for the advantage of the organization.

Workers should not have an undue amount of time taken from their duties to write reports or attend review conferences. Furthermore, the reports that are expected of workers should involve information that they themselves can use. The well-planned report form will be an aid to both workers and the leader.

Methods of Control

Control methods may differ according to the size and complexity of the organization. In smaller churches, a great deal of control can be done through personal contact. The pastor and his department leaders may be in a position to evaluate the activities through personal observation. While there are obvious benefits in having firsthand information, this kind of control may produce a negative reaction because it makes the workers think the pastor or leader is constantly looking over their shoulders. Control of this sort must be done with discretion.

In larger churches, management control is often accomplished by lay leaders who report only those situations that are not on schedule or are in trouble. The pastor can assume that anything not reported is on target. Only the troublesome areas come to the attention of the manager.

Another method is known as point control, which relies upon the immediate supervisor to control problems in his respective area of responsibility. An example would be the pastor's reliance upon the youth director to take care of problems arising from the youth activities. Such matters would not reach the pastor and thus would not overload him with unnecessary details. This type of control places great confidence in the subordinate leaders and can only work if they are competent.

Collecting Information

In collecting and recording data, the same types of information should be used from year to year so that comparisons can be made. In some areas, the only concern is the quantitative total; other records may deal with averages. In order to have clear comparisons, we must be talking about the same kind of data. Creative type ministries will require broader performance standards without too much definition of specific functions. Performance standards can be established from previous experience and appraisals. They do not necessarily imply perfection and may sometimes reflect average, acceptable service. The PERT chart considered in Chapter Two may also be used as an important control device. The manager can make a quick evaluation and then take action to speed up the phases that are lagging.

Remedial Action

Good management principles assume that workers have a right to know how well they are doing in relationship to their goals. Reports and evaluations are intended to lead to remedial action. The pastor should develop a trustful atmosphere which makes it possible for him to speak frankly to his people. If the workers know that the pastor really cares for them, they will be more inclined to follow his directions for improvement. There are many times when control can be accomplished only by person-to-person conferences with objective evaluation.

Frequently the difficulty lies in ineffective methods. Since the wise controller sees methods as means to an end, he will not hesitate to change methods to improve achievement.

Sometimes failure may be the result of poor spiritual life. In this case, the pastor is controlling when he counsels the worker and leads him back into a renewed relationship with the Lord.

Then, too, policies and practices may need to be reviewed to produce greater effectiveness. There is no end to the need for updating.

Occasionally service is hindered when a worker has been assigned too many tasks. An overloaded church worker may end up accomplishing none of his tasks.

Corrective action comes only when the workers understand their responsibilities and accept the standards agreed on by the group. Each worker in the church needs to know exactly what is expected of him. No one can be held accountable for failure resulting from circumstances beyond his control such as bad weather conditions or severe, widespread illness.

Discipline is another form of control. Spiritual integrity and holy living are basic ingredients of Christian living. If the pastor sees careless conduct, he will need to resort to some kind of corrective discipline. Whenever discipline is imposed, it should only be after thorough investigation. When the violation is serious, the *Manual* provides for a local board of discipline to handle such matters. Discipline should be applied kindly, lovingly, but firmly.

Financial control is perhaps one of the easiest areas of management. Local church budgets should be well planned with financial records, report forms, and year-to-date charts set up to complement the budget form. Financial trends should be interpreted and necessary budget adjustments made. If the pastor has adequate control, he can tell when to expand his program and when to slow down certain projects. Adequate financial control will help coordinate the work, fix responsibility, reduce waste, and help the church to operate more efficiently.

Control Forms

Keep report forms relevant to needs and adjust them to changing conditions. Strive for a minimum number and a simplified structure. Before another form is introduced, an older one probably ought to be discontinued.

Appendix F has examples of a number of different types of forms which a local church could use to advantage as control tools.

Epilogue

So you are a pastor. You have the most influential assignment in the church. You have a golden opportunity to build good people and a great church. But the chances of blundering into success in today's pastoral ministry are slim. Being a pastor is more than having a pulpit, a stained-glass voice, and a black suit. As you know, the pastorate makes many demands upon a man—demands of character, drive, and health. He must know the Bible, God, people, and his world. He must thoroughly understand his mission, preach the Word, make sound judgments, and direct the work of many people.

The Royal Bank of Canada challenged her executives with these marks of a "pro":

1. He does not accept mediocrity.

2. He continues his education so as to keep his performance up-to-date.

3. He accepts the ethical rules of the game.

4. He keeps looking for better ways to do things.

5. He is open-minded.

6. He is fair in his dealings with people.[*]

That list is only a beginning for creative pastoral managers. The continuing task of church development is before us. It is worthy of our best, and the development of good management skills will increase the effectiveness of our ministry—all for His glory.

---

[*]*Of Interest to Executives* (Montreal, Que.: The Royal Bank of Canada, 1971).

Appendix A

LOCAL CHURCH ORGANIZATION CHART

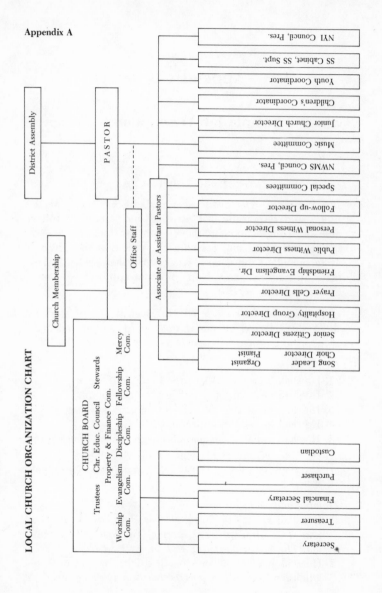

District Assembly

PASTOR

Church Membership

Office Staff

Associate or Assistant Pastors

CHURCH BOARD
Trustees Chr. Educ. Council Stewards
Property & Finance Com.
Worship Evangelism Discipleship Fellowship Mercy
Com.   Com.   Com.   Com.   Com.

NYI Council, Pres.
SS Cabinet, SS Supt.
Youth Coordinator
Children's Coordinator
Junior Church Director
Music Committee
NWMS Council, Pres.
Special Committees
Follow-up Director
Personal Witness Director
Public Witness Director
Friendship Evangelism Dir.
Prayer Cells Director
Hospitality Group Director
Senior Citizens Director
Song Leader Choir Director Pianist
Organist
Custodian
Purchaser
Financial Secretary
Treasurer
Secretary

Appendix B

Sample Job Description

Date _____

Head Usher

I. *Job Summary.* The head usher shall be in charge of the ushers and responsible for assisting and making comfortable the congregation in the church building, for receiving the offerings, and assisting the pastor in the physical arrangement of the church service. He shall seek to eliminate distractions and help provide appropriate conditions for church services.

II. *Organizational Relationships.* He shall be nominated by the pastor, elected by the church board, and be accountable to the pastor.

III. *Qualifications.*
1. He shall be a member of the local church.
2. He shall be exemplary in Christian conduct.
3. He shall be at least 25 years of age and not over 70.
4. He shall be neat in appearance.
5. He shall radiate Christian cheer, grace, and courtesy.
6. He shall be regular in church service attendance.
7. He shall be able to lead and supervise subordinate ushers.

IV. *Training and Development*
1. He shall read *The Story of Ourselves,* by A. F. Harper; *The Ministry of Ushering,* by Mark R. Moore; and *The Usher and How to Ush,* by Ron Lush.
2. He will read such books and articles on personal relationships and ushering as the pastor may recommend.

V. *Duties*
  1. He shall recommend to the pastor men to be considered for the office of usher.
  2. He shall supervise the ushers and establish schedules and places for their service.
  3. He shall advise the assistant head usher of any anticipated absence in time to see that the office duties are covered.
  4. He shall see that worshippers are properly seated, giving special assistance to visitors.
  5. He shall see that visitors' cards are given to all first-time visitors.
  6. He shall see that Sunday bulletins and other materials are distributed as directed by the pastor.
  7. He shall see that comfortable temperatures are maintained and the lighting is provided as requested by the pastor.
  8. He shall endeavor to meet any emergency needs of the people and attempt to keep proper order. He shall call for emergency assistance when needed.
  9. He shall see that all offerings are deposited in the financial secretary's office and placed in safekeeping.
  10. He shall see that adequate ushers' supplies, including visitors' cards, brochures, badges, reservation signs, offering envelopes, and offering plates are maintained and kept neatly in the ushers' closet and that requisitions are made for replacements.
  11. He shall see that attendance counts are taken in all services and recorded in the attendance record book in the church office.

Appendix C

Agenda for Local Board Meetings

Date _____

1. Call to Order
2. Scripture and Prayer
3. Roll Call
4. Approval of Minutes
5. Pastor's Report
6. Treasurer's Report
7. Department Leaders' Reports
   a. Sunday School Superintendent
   b. NYI President
   c. NWMS President
8. Standing Committee Reports

   a. Trustees
   b. Stewards   —OR—
   c. Education Committee

   a. Worship
   b. Evangelism
   c. Discipleship
   d. Fellowship
   e. Mercy
   f. Finance
   g. Property

9. Special Committee Reports
10. Miscellaneous Old Business
11. Miscellaneous New Business
12. Adjournment

Appendix D

Planning a Church Budget

There are various ways to make up a budget. The size of the church will dictate how detailed or complex it needs to be. The simplest form is to start out with an estimate of the amount of money which will be raised for all purposes in the coming year. Next write down all the fixed items of expenditure (salaries, budgets, building payments, etc.), and distribute the remainder over anticipated needs and projected programs in the various phases of the church's activities (music, maintenance, office expense, revivals, utilities, equipment, etc.).

Another approach is to work from needs or anticipated expenditures and from that determine what amount will have to be raised to meet the total needs. This amount should be realistic but be a challenge to the stewardship of the congregation. (The budget plan outlined below in Appendix E basically follows this latter procedure.)

It has been suggested that the pastor set up the pilot budget. Sometimes the finance committee or an appointed budget committee is given this responsibility. The latter arrangement avoids the awkward situation when salary considerations enter in. In any case, the pastor needs to be involved closely in budget planning.

The sample budget in Appendix E further assumes that the church has a unified budget which incorporates not only the finances of the church itself but also its auxiliaries (Sunday school, NYI, NWMS, etc.). In this method (which is highly recommended), the treasurers of the various departments keep detailed records, but the money goes through the church treasury and is disbursed from there.

The instructions for making up a budget like Appendix E

are given below. It is more detailed than many churches require, but the basic principles apply to a church of any size.

We start with category number 1 in the Disbursements section, the Local Operational Fund (LOF), writing in figures for anticipated "A. Material" costs in the numerous subdivisions, such as utilities, telephone, taxes, and insurance. Items 1-18 are then added up to give the total material cost on line A.

Next, B items (Staff Expenses) are considered, and anticipated salaries, financial benefits, parsonage costs, car allowance, and guest speakers are written in. These 18 items all add up to total Staff Expenses.

Item C is the Contingent Fund, which is an estimate to cover all unexpected and nonbudgeted expenses and perhaps allow for some shortage of income. The contingent fund may run as much as 10 percent of the total budget. Most churches, however, have not reached this ideal, and the sample budget shows only $2,500 in the contingent fund as compared to the total budget of $64,471. Thus contingent fund, staff expenses, and material make up the total local operational fund.

The Giving to Others (Denominational Budgets) is easy to figure. If the district ways and means committee has a regular formula for figuring all of the budgets, that may be applied to the projection of the local church's income for the present year. This will at least come close to the budgets which will be assigned at the coming district assembly. In local church budget planning, provision should be made that following the district assembly, the budget may be adjusted to state the actual budget figures assigned to the church.

The plan here shows that budgets would be paid from the main church organization rather than the auxiliaries of Sunday school, NYI, or NWMS. The only exception suggested is that the NWMS may plan to make a substantial contribution to the General Budget through Prayer and Self-denial offerings. Parts of the Easter and Thanksgiving offerings or the annual missionary conference may also be credited to the NWMS. Thus in listing the figures for General Budget, the total General Budget may be written in parentheses on line A, but only that anticipated amount of the General Budget paid by the church, exclusive of the NWMS resources, should be entered on the General Budget line. Thus all of the denominational budgets paid by the main church treasure will be listed on category number 2.

Building Fund and Debt Reduction (category number 3) lists mortgage payments. Space is given for more than one mortgage so that total mortgage payments are entered.

Category number 4 deals with Building Maintenance and is frequently overlooked in local budgets. So long as the church owns property, it will have to be maintained. Such maintenance as repairing of broken windows, small redecorating jobs, repair of plumbing, heating, air conditioning, and carpentry will be included on line 4A. Line item 4B (Capital Improvements) should cover long-range, major building improvements, such as total exterior painting, new roof, new heating system, new air conditioning system, major landscaping, parking lot paving, and construction or alteration that materially increases the value of the property. By keeping these two categories separate, a pastor will budget for current maintenance needs plus providing for major improvements that may be a year or more in the future. Capital investment maintenance money may be allocated and saved over a period of months or years towards the eventual payment of major renovations.

Category number 5 (Evangelism) provides funding for revivals and evangelistic meetings, visitation crusades, and literature distribution. The line item 5A through 5G will add up to the total special evangelism costs.

Category 6 has to do with Special Benevolences. These may include offerings for Nazarene Theological Seminary, Nazarene Bible College, American Bible Society (which is sometimes sponsored by the church), local ministerial associations, and various community projects. In the sample only three such special interests are listed. Often special offerings are taken for these interests, but having them in the budget at least gives goals for such items.

Categories number 7, 8, and 9 have to do with the various Sunday school, NYI, and NWMS expenses. Notice line items C and D in the NWMS section concerning General Budget, Easter and Thanksgiving offerings. If these offerings are received as NWMS projects, they should be counted here.

Category number 10 (Designated Funds) includes such items as General Assembly Reserve, Memorial Funds, scholarships, or even capital investment or relocation. It is a listing of special funds that may be used only for the designated purposes. Frequently designated funds are raised in one year but not spent until later years. For instance, the church may set aside General Assembly funds each year but disburse them only once every four years. These designated funds should not be budgeted as expenditures in that year but rather be held in reserve. The budget line items will then not be in balance unless the items being held are shown both as an add item and a subtraction item (in parentheses). When done this way, the total will balance with the total receipts.

Category number 11 (Special Enterprises) is left open and could be the budget portion for any projects not included in other categories.

The total disbursement categories are then added together to produce the grand total of disbursements. This is the anticipated amount needed to operate the church's program.

To complete the budget, we must now go back to the Receipts section and write in the same category totals as were set in the disbursements. For instance, category 1 (Local Operational Funds) in disbursements is $25,570. On the receipt side of the budget under 1 (LOF), the figure $25,570 should be written in. This should be done in all the categories, finally writing into the total receipts the same figure as given for total disbursements, $64,471. Now we begin with receipt items, working in reverse from category 11 or 10 back to category number 1.

In Receipts category number 10 (Designated Funds), we now know that $1,600 must be planned in receipts to meet the designated disbursement items. In this hypothetical church, let us suppose designated funds are all transferred from the income of tithes and offerings. Thus on line 10A, $200 is recorded as transferred from Operational Fund for General Assembly Reserve. On line 10B, $200 is written in as transferred from local operational fund for a college scholarship; and on line 10C, $1,200 is written in as transferred from local operational fund for capital investment. These line items then add up to $1,600. Now, because these funds are transferred, we will move over to Receipts category item number 1 (Local Operational Fund). On line 1K (Transferred to Designated Funds), we will write in $1,600, which is in parentheses. The parentheses indicate that the amount contained is *subtracted* from the list of line items. Also, to assist the treasurer in making transfers, $133.33, which is 1/12 of the annual $1,600, is written in as the amount for the monthly transfer.

On Receipts category 9, we know we must receive $4,295 in order to balance the NWMS budget. We decide that $1,170 may come in through Prayer and Self-denial, $100 may come in through deputation offerings for visiting missionaries, $25.00 may be received for the language broadcast offerings, $500 may come in through Alabaster offerings, and $1,950 may come in as offerings for the special NWMS projects. This leaves $550 which will have to come in through local chapter offerings. Since ordinarily there will be 12 missionary meetings per year, this means that monthly offerings must average $45.83.

In category 8 (NYI), our budget shows that we need $400. This can be raised by $175 in Youth Week offerings and $225 in weekly offerings which would have to average $5.36 for 42 Sundays.

In the Sunday school category (number 7) the amount is $1,645. It is planned that $150 will come in through Caravan offerings. This leaves a balance of $1,495 to be received in Sunday school offerings, which would need to average $28.75 per Sunday.

The Special Interest category (number 6) calls for $95.00. This is to be made up by $35.00 for Nazarene Bible College, $35.00 for Nazarene Theological Seminary, and $25.00 for American Bible Society.

The evangelism category (number 5) has a budget of $2,400. It is estimated that $1,000 can be received from offerings during the revival meetings. The regular Wednesday night offerings, according to this adopted budget, are to be used for the evangelism budget item. We can expect 36 such Wednesday night offerings through the year, which would need to total $540. In order to meet the evangelism goal, $410 will have to be transferred from the Operational Fund. This amount is written in here as a receipt. Immediately we turn to Receipts, category number 1 (LOF) and line item 1G and write in the same $410 in parentheses. This indicates the transfer and the $410 is subtracted from the total column. The treasurer is thus directed to transfer $34.17 per month from the local operational fund to evangelism. Thus the line items equal the special category budget of $2,400.

Building Maintenance (category 4) is set at $1,900. Since there are no special offerings or income for building maintenance, the entire amount will be transferred from local operational funds. Thus we are writing in on line 4A for current maintenance, $1,100, and on line 4B for capital improvements, $800. The total is $1,900. Since this is a transfer, we immediately go to category 1 (LOF) and line item 1F and write in the parentheses $1,900, which is to be subtracted from the local operational fund. The treasurer will also be guided in transfers by the indication that $158.33 per month is to be transferred from the local operational fund to building maintenance.

Category number 3 (Building Fund and Debt Reduction) totals $3,780. It is estimated that the church will receive $2,400 in the year for building fund offerings. That leaves a deficit of $1,380 that must be transferred from local operational funds. Thus, $1,380 is written in on line 3A. But immediately we move to category number 1 (LOF) and on line 1E write in $1,380 in parentheses, which indicates the amount to be subtracted from local operational funds. The treasurer is guided by the note that $115 per month should be transferred from the local operational fund to debt reduction (item 3).

We go now to category number 2 (Giving for Others— Denominational Budgets), which calls for a total of $9,286. Since in our sample we did not count the Easter and Thanksgiving offerings for General Budget under NWMS, we may count them here. It is estimated that this church will raise $1,000 each in Thanksgiving and Easter offerings for a total of $2,000 during the year for General Budget. This leaves a deficit of $7,286, which must be transferred from the tithes (1A) that come in through local operational funds. So on line 2A we write in the amount to be transferred from the operational fund, $7,286. We move immediately to the local operational fund, and on line 1D (transferred to denominational budgets) we write in the total $7,286. This is again put in parentheses, indicating it is subtracted from the total amount received in this category. The treasurer will be guided by the figure that calls for a transfer from the operational fund to denominational budgets of $607.17 per month. This kind of budgeting, along with the transfers, will assure regular and sufficient payments on all denominational budgets (assuming the income of the church is equal to the total budget expectation).

Finally, we move to category number 1 (Operational Fund), which calls for a total of $25,570. Lines 1E and 1F provide possible listings of other incomes into the local operational fund that are not anticipated in the budget. Line item 1D (Interest) is an estimate of interest received by the church on its savings accounts during the year. Line item 1C includes offerings that would be taken in junior church which, in this case, are estimated at $150. Line item 1B would be the midweek offerings; however, in this budget they have already been assigned to evangelism so do not appear here.

95

Line item 1A is the critical item in the budget. It is the last one to be figured and indeed the most important. We arrive at the amount of tithes and loose offerings which will be needed by simply starting with the Local Operational Fund amount needed ($25,570), subtracting the interest of $50.00, adding all the transferred items ($12,576), and subtracting junior church offerings and midweek offerings. The net amount is $37,946. This is what must be raised to cover the budget for this year. We determine that such a goal would require an average Sunday offering of $729.73.

If the pastor sees that the average budgeted Sunday offering is too high to be realistic, he must then go back through the budget of disbursements and reduce certain line items accordingly. This would call for a reduction of total disbursements and the equalizing of such by reducing the line item receipts of tithes and loose offerings. On the other hand, if the budgeted average Sunday offerings is below what might be expected, he may then reverse the procedure by adding to the disbursements at certain points. This would increase the budgeted amount of tithes and offerings needed.

The pastor or budget committee now has an adequate budget plan which can be submitted to the finance committee for their review and revisions. The revised budget may then be presented to the church board for adoption. This budget form not only helps in planning but provides a control document.

A slightly modified section form of this church budget will be needed by churches using the Faith-Promise program in which an annual pledge is received for missions. The changes occur only on categories 2 and 9, which cover denominational budgets and NWMS. It simply would provide for money received by annual pledges rather than through the many NWMS items (9A-9I).

Appendix E

Annual Church Budget Form

Year _____

RECEIPTS:

1. Local Operational Fund (LOF) .... $*25,570*

    A. Tithes and offerings .... $*31,946*
        (average per Sunday $*729.73*)
    B. Midweek offerings ....   _____
    C. Junior church offerings *150*
    D. Interest *50*
    E. _____   _____
    F. _____   _____

Transferred to Other Funds:

    G. Transferred to
        Denominational Budgets ....   (*7,286*)
        ($*607.17* per month)
    H. Transferred to Building Fund
        & Debt Reduction ....   (*1,380*)
        ($*115.00* per month)
    I. Transferred to Building
       Maintenance ....   (*1,900*)
       ($*158.33* per month)
    J. Transferred to Special
       Evangelism ....   (*410*)
       ($*34.17* per month)
    K. Transferred to Designated
        Funds ....   (*1,600*) (*12,576*)
        ($*133.33* per month)

2. Giving to Others—Denominational Budgets *9,286*

   A. Transferred from Operational
      Fund *7,286*
   B. Easter Offering—General
      Budget (if not in NWMS) *1,000*
   C. Thanksgiving Offering—
      General Budget (if not in
      NWMS) *1,000*
   D. _____ ____
   E. _____ ____

3. Building Fund and Debt Reduction *3,780*

   A. Transferred from Operational
      Fund *1,380*
   B. Building Fund offerings *2,400*
   C. _____ ____
   D. _____ ____

4. Building Maintenance *1,900*

   A. Transferred from LOF for
      current maintenance *1,100*
   B. Transferred from LOF for
      capital improvement *800*
   C. _____ ____

5. Evangelism *2,400*

   A. Transferred from Operational
      Fund *410*
   B. Offerings *1,000*
   C. Midweek offerings (if not
      counted in Local Operational
      Fund) *540*
   D. Special event offerings *250*
   E. Literature Fund *200*
   F. _____ ____

6. Special Interests .... _95_

   A. Nazarene Theological
      Seminary .... _35_
   B. Nazarene Bible College .... _35_
   C. American Bible Society .... _25_
   D. _____ ____

7. Sunday School .... _1,645_

   A. Sunday offerings .... _1,495_
      (average per Sunday $_28.75_)
   B. Caravan .... _150_
   C. _____ ____
   D. _____ ____
   E. _____ ____

8. NYI .... _400_

   A. Sunday offerings .... _225_
      (average for _42_ Sundays
      $_5.36_)
   B. Youth Week offerings .... _175_
   C. _____ ____

9. NWMS .... _4,295_

   A. Prayer and Self-denial dues ..... _1,170_
   B. Annual Faith-Promise
      Pledges .... ____
   C. Easter Offering, General
      Budget .... ____
   D. Thanksgiving Offering,
      General Budget .... ____
   E. Special Project Offering .... _1,950_
   F. Alabaster Offerings .... _500_
   G. Deputation Offerings .... _100_
   H. Language Offering .... _25_
   I. Local Chapter Offering .... _550_
   J. Local Convention Offering ...... ____
   K. _____ ____

10. Designated Funds *1,600*

   A. Transferred from Operational
      Fund, for General Assembly
      Reserve *200*
   B. Transferred from LOF for
      College Scholarship *200*
   C. Transferred from LOF for
      Capital Investment *1,200*
   D. Memorial Fund .... ——
   E. _____ ——

11. Special Enterprises—Day-Care Center *13,500*

   A. _____ ——
   B. _____ ——
   C. _____ ——

      Total Receipts .... $*64,471*

DISBURSEMENTS

1. Local Operational Fund *25,570*

   A. Material .... —— *4,725*

      1. Church utilities *4,100*
      2. Church telephone *350*
      3. Taxes *115*
      4. Church insurance *250*
      5. Advertising *400*
      6. Postage *350*
      7. Office supplies *600*
      8. Program materials *500*
      9. Equipment, furnishings *700*
      10. Custodial supplies *150*
      11. Nursery supplies,
          equipment *100*
      12. Flowers *110*

13. _____ ____
14. _____ ____
15. _____ ____
16. _____ ____
17. _____ ____
18. _____ ____

B. Staff Expenses .... ____ *18,345*

   1. Pastor's salary *9,620*
   2. Ass't pastor's salary .... ____
   3. Social Security
      reimbursement *900*
   4. Annuity *480*
   5. Health insurance
      premiums *680*
   6. Custodian's salary *1,040*
   7. Secretarial wages *2,750*
   8. Parsonage utilities (1) *900*
   9. Parsonage utilities (2) .... ____
  10. Parsonage telephone (1) *275*
  11. Parsonage telephone (2) ..... ____
  12. Parsonage furnishings *400*
  13. Pastor's car allowance *780*
  14. Pastor's convention
       expenses *100*
  15. Guest speakers *120*
  16. District Assembly *150*
  17. Continuing Education *150*
  18. _____ ____
  19. _____ ____
  20. _____ ____
  21. _____ ____

C. Contingent Fund .... ____ *2,500*

   1. _____ ____
   2. _____ ____

2. Giving to Others—Denominational Budgets *9,286*

   A. General Budget—paid by
      church *3,276*
   B. District Budget *4,210*
   C. College Budget *850*
   D. Pensions *695*
   E. Camp *255*
   F. Zone College .... ____
   G. _____ ____

3. Building Fund and Debt Reduction *3,780*

   A. Mortgage payments (1) *3,780*
   B. Mortgage payments (2) .... ____
   C. _____ ____
   D. _____ ____

4. Building Maintenance *4,900*

   A. Current maintenance *4,100*
   B. Capital improvements *800*

5. Evangelism *3,400*

   A. Evangelist's honorarium *800*
   B. Meeting expenses *300*
   C. Literature, subscriptions *650*
   D. Visitation supplies *100*
   E. Evangelist's Soc. Sec., travel,
      hospital, benefits *300*
   F. Special events *250*
   G. _____ ____

6. Special Benevolences *95*

   A. Nazarene Theological
      Seminary *35*
   B. Nazarene Bible College *35*
   C. American Bible Society *25*
   D. _____ ____

7. Sunday School *4645*

    A. Local expenses *4375*
    B. District dues *60*
    C. Caravan *150*
    D. District convention *60*
    E. _____ ———
    F. _____ ———

8. NYI *400*

    A. Local expenses *90*
    B. District dues *85*
    C. Youth Week *175*
    D. District convention *50*
    E. _____ ———
    F. _____ ———

9. NWMS *7,295*

    A. General Budget—Prayer &
       Self-denial *4170*
    B. General Budget .... ———
    C. General Budget—Easter
       Offering .... ———
    D. General Budget—Thanksgiving
       Offering .... ———
    E. Special Project *4950*
    F. Alabaster *500*
    G. Deputation *100*
    H. Latin Language Broadcast *25*
    I. Local chapter expenses *75*
    J. Local convention expenses ...... ———
    K. District dues *100*
    L. General expense *40*
    M. Medical Aid *60*
    N. Box Work *25*
    O. Memorial Roll *50*

P. Special missionary
   promotion *125*
Q. District convention *75*
R. _____ —
S. _____ —
T. _____ —

10. Designated Funds *200*

A. General Assembly *200*
   Held in reserve .... (*200*)
B. College scholarship *200*
   Held in reserve .... (—)
C. Capital investment *4,200*
   Held in reserve .... (*4,200*)
D. College scholarship .... —
   Held in reserve .... (—)
E. _____ —
   Held in reserve .... (—)

11. Special Enterprises—Day-Care Center *13,500*

A. _____ —
B. _____ —
C. _____ —

   Total Disbursements .... $*63,071*

Reserve Funds .... $*4,400*

A. General Assembly
   Fund *200*
B. _____ —
C. Capital Investment *4,200*
D. _____ —
E. _____ —
F. _____ —
G. _____ —

   Total Disbursements and Reserve .... $*64,471*

Appendix F

Forms

Pastor's Monthly Report to the Church Board

Month of _____ 19___

1. *Membership*
   a. New members _____
   b. Members dropped _____
   c. Current membership _____

2. *Rituals*
   a. Communion services _____
   b. Baptisms _____
   c. Dedications _____
   d. Weddings _____
   e. Funerals _____

3. *Attendance*
   a. Average Sunday morning _____
   b. Average Sunday evening _____
   c. Average Wednesday evening _____

4. *Finance*
   a. Total receipts _____
   b. Average weekly tithe receipts _____

5. *Year-to-date Statistics*

Item	Goal	This Year	Last Year
a. Church membership	_____	_____	_____
b. Received by prof. of faith	_____	_____	_____
c. New converts	_____	_____	_____
d. New prospects	_____	_____	_____
e. Sunday morning average	_____	_____	_____
f. Sunday evening average	_____	_____	_____
g. Wednesday evening average	_____	_____	_____
h. Sunday school average	_____	_____	_____

i. NYI average .... _____ _____ _____
j. First-time visitors .... _____ _____ _____
k. Weekly tithes receipts .... _____ _____ _____
l. Faith-Promise receipts
    (or Missions) .... _____ _____ _____
m.(Building Fund receipts) .... _____ _____ _____
n. (Special Fund) .... _____ _____ _____
6. Pastoral Activities:

7. State of the Church (comments and recommendations):

Signed: _____

Sunday School Superintendent's Report

Month of _____ 19_____
1. Enrollment and Attendance (Monthly average)

	Enrollment		Attendance	
Departments	This Year	Last Year	This Year	Last Year
_____	___	___	___	___
_____	___	___	___	___
_____	___	___	___	___
_____	___	___	___	___
_____	___	___	___	___
_____	___	___	___	___
_____	___	___	___	___
Officers, teachers	___	___	___	___

106

	This Year	*Last Year*
Active membership	_____	_____
Cradle Roll	_____	_____
Home Department	_____	_____
Outreach	_____	_____
Total Enrollment	_____	_____
New members enrolled	_____	
Members dropped	_____	

2. Finances:

   Last month's balance .... $ _____   Average Sunday

   Offerings received .... _____   Offering:

   Total to account for .... $ _____

   Disbursements .... _____ $ _____

   Balance carried forward .... $ _____

3. Visitation: absentee calls _____; prospect calls _____;
   new contact calls _____; survey homes contacted _____.

4. Christian Service Training credits earned _____

5. Teachers involved in teacher training course _____
   Registered teachers _____; Qualified _____; Certified _____.

6. District dues paid to date $_____. Balance due $_____.

7. Special programs conducted:

8. Personnel needs:

9. Equipment needs:

Signed: _____

NWMS President's Report

1. Total membership _____ Active _____ Associate _____
   Junior _____ Teen _____ Adults _____
2. Number of meetings (total of all chapters) _____
   Junior _____ Teen _____ Adults _____
3. Average attendance (total) _____ Last year _____
   Junior _____ Teen _____ Adults _____
4. Total missionary offerings received in church and NWMS
   $_____ Total last year $_____
5. Number of Prayer and Self-denial members _____
   (goal _____)
6. Reading books completed, all chapters _____
   (goal _____)
7. *World Mission* subscriptions _____ (goal _____)
8. Box Work activities:

9. Other projects:

10. Special programs held:

11. Special programs planned:

Signed: _____

108

NYI President's Report

Month of _____ 19____

1. Membership total _____
   Junior _____ Teen _____ Y.A. _____
   added _____ dropped _____
2. Average Attendance _____
   Junior _____ Teen _____ Y.A. _____
3. Devotional meetings held
   Junior _____ Teen _____ Y.A. _____
4. *Bread* subscriptions _____ *Etcetera* subscriptions _____
5. Financial report:
   Balance from last month .... $ _____
   Month's receipts .... _____
   Total to account for .... $ _____
   Disbursements .... _____
   Balance carried forward .... $ _____
6. District dues paid $_____ Balance due $_____
7. Special programs held (Youth Week, summer camps, District Convention, District Bible Quizzing, District Talent Contest, zone rallies, etc.)

8. Comments and recommendations:

Signed: _____

109

Church Treasurer's Report*

Month of _____ 19_____

RECEIPTS:

1. Local Operational Fund $3,026.10

    A. Tithes and offerings .... $ 3,062.10
       (average per Sunday $765.53)
    B. Midweek offerings .... _____
    C. Junior church offerings .... _____12.00
    D. Transferred to Denominational
       Budgets ....⟍... (607.17)
    E. Transferred to Building Fund &
       Debt Reduction .... (115.00)
    F. Transferred to Building
       Maintenance .... (158.33)
    G. Transferred to Special
       Evangelism .... (34.17)
    H. Transferred to Designated Funds ... (133.33)
    I. Interest .... _____
    J. _____ _____

2. Giving to Others—Denominational Budgets 4,722.47

    A. Transferred from Operational
       Fund 607.17
    B. Easter Offering—General Budget
       (if not in NWMS) 4,115.30
    C. Thanksgiving Offering—General
       Budget (if not in NWMS) ....
    D. _____ _____
    E. _____ _____

3. Building Fund 300.00

    A. Transferred from Operational
       Fund 115.00
    B. Building Fund offerings 185.00
    C. _____ _____

*See Appendix E (budget form) for explanation.

110

4. Building Maintenance .... _156.33_

   A. Transferred from LOF for current
      maintenance .... _91.67_
   B. Transferred from LOF for capital
      improvements .... _66.66_
   C. _____ _____

5. Evangelism .... _428.65_

   A. Transferred from Operational
      Fund .... _34.17_
   B. Offerings .... _345.00_
   C. Midweek offerings (if not
      counted in Local Operational
      Fund .... _46.48_
   D. Special event offering .... _____
   E. Literature Fund .... _3.00_
   F. _____ _____

6. Special Interests .... _5.00_

   A. Nazarene Theological Seminary .... _5.00_
   B. _____ _____
   C. _____ _____
   D. _____ _____

7. Sunday School .... _73.61_

8. NYI .... _13.93_

9. NWMS .... _61.31_

10. Designated Funds .... _133.33_

   A. General Assembly Reserve .... _16.67_
   B. College Scholarship Fund .... _16.66_
   C. Capital Investment .... _100.00_
   D. Memorial Fund .... _____

11. Special Enterprises—Day-Care Center .... _1,319.00_

Total Receipts .... $_6,241.73_

DISBURSEMENTS:

1. Local Operational Fund .... $ *4,657.13*

    A. Material .... _____ $ *407.21*
        1. Church utilities .... $ *84.30*
        2. Church telephone .... _____
        3. Taxes .... _____
        4. Church insurance *124.16*
        5. Advertising ....
        6. Postage .... _____
        7. Office supplies .... _____
        8. Program materials *198.75*
        9. Equipment, furnishings ....
        10. Custodial supplies .... _____
        11. Nursery supplies, equipment .... _____
        12. Flowers .... _____
        13. _____ _____
        14. _____ _____
        15. _____ _____

    B. Staff Expenses .... _____ *4,249.92*

        1. Pastor's salary *740.00*
        2. Ass't pastor's salary .... _____
        3. Social Security
           reimbursement *75.00*
        4. Annuity .... _____
        5. Health insurance premiums *56.67*
        6. Custodian's salary *86.67*
        7. Secretarial wages *220.00*
        8. Parsonage utilities (1) *24.70*
        9. Parsonage utilities (2) ....
        10. Parsonage telephone (1) .... *(13.12)*
        11. Parsonage telephone (2) ....
        12. Parsonage furnishings ....
        13. Pastor's car allowance *60.00*
        14. Pastor's convention expense .....
        15. Guest speakers ....
        16. District Assembly ....
        17. Continuing Education ....
        18. _____ _____
        19. _____ _____
        20. _____ _____

C. Contingent Fund .... _____
   1. _____ _____
   2. _____ _____

2. Giving to Others—Denominational Budgets *1,889.13*
  A. General Budget, paid by church *4,388.30*
  B. District Budget *350.83*
  C. College Budget *70.83*
  D. Pensions *57.92*
  E. Camp *21.25*
  F. _____ _____
  G. _____ _____

3. Building Fund and Debt Reduction *315.00*
  A. Mortgage payments (1) *315.00*
  B. Mortgage payments (2) .... _____
  C. _____ _____

4. Building Maintenance *142.70*
  A. Current maintenance *142.70*
  B. Capital improvements .... _____

5. Evangelism *258.22*
  A. Evangelist's honorarium *210.00*
  B. Meeting expenses *48.22*
  C. Literature, subscriptions .... _____
  D. Visitation supplies .... _____
  E. Evangelist's Soc. Sec., travel,
     benefits .... _____
  F. Special events .... _____
  G. _____ _____

6. Special Benevolences *5.00*
  A. Nazarene Theological Seminary *5.00*
  B. _____ _____
  C. _____ _____
  D. _____ _____

7. Sunday School *83.65*

8. NYI *36.90*

9. NWMS .... _76 40_

10. Designated Funds .... ———
    A. _____ ———
    B. _____ ———
    C. _____ ———
    D. _____ ———

11. Special Enterprises—Day-Care Center .... _742.75_

    Total Disbursements .... $_5206.88_

ANALYSIS:

  A. Balance at beginning of month ...... $ _5,966.64_
  B. Receipts for the month .... _6,241.73_
  C. Total to account for .... _12,208.37_
  D. Total disbursements .... _5,206.88_
  E. Balance at end of month .... _7,001.49_
  F. Analysis of Balance
    1. Local Operational Fund .... $ _4,617.92_
    2. Giving to Others—
      Denominational Budgets .... (_166.66_)
    3. Building Fund and Debt
      Reduction .... _105.00_
    4. Building Maintenance .... _488.92_
    5. Evangelism .... _553.57_
    6. Special Interests .... ———
    7. Sunday School .... _753.87_
    8. NYI .... _84.17_
    9. NWMS .... _52.12_
    10. Designated Funds .... _2,563.33_
    11. Special Enterprises—Day-Care
      Center .... _949.25_
  G. Balance Deposited:
    Checking account .... $ _800.00_
    Savings account .... _6,201.49_
  H. Balance carried forward less
    outstanding accounts. (List
    attached) .... $ _24.95_
  I. Principal balance of property
    indebtedness .... $ _6,976.54_

J. Budget Status to date:

	Paid	As-signed	Bal-ance
General Budget			
Paid by church $ 4,388.30			
Paid by NWMS _____			
Total	$ 4,388.30	$ 4,446.00	$ 3,057.70
District Budget	350.83	4,210.00	3,859.17
College Budget	70.83	850.00	779.17
Camp Budget	21.25	225.00	203.75
Pensions Budget	57.92	695.00	637.08

Attendance Record

Year _____

Week of	Sun. a.m.	Sun. p.m.	Wed.	SS	NYI	NWMS	Revival	Other
Apr. 6	237	145		237	52	76		
13	316	111	80	287	54			
20	270	181	75	274	59			
27	251	158	87	244	91			
Average	-269-	-149-	-81-	-261-	-64-			
May 4	253	172		269	54	73		
11	245	137	80	240	80			
18	271	171	79	275	51			
25	261	132	80	242	39			
Average	-258-	153-	-80-	-257-	-56-			
June 1	286	184		260	123	75		
8	259	159	74	233	47			
15	232	123	82	244	43			
22	200	123	79	215	39			
29	186	90		190	51			
Average	-233-	-136-	-78-	-228-	-60-			

(This chart shows a three-month period, but the entire year would be recorded following this same procedure.)

115

Record of Offerings

Year ――――――

Week of	Total	Tithes & Offerings	Junior Church	Building Fund	Midweek	Sun. Sch.	NYI	NWMS or Missions	Other
Apr. 6	$1,966.07	$ 738.20	$ 3.09	$ 50.00	$15.10	$16.41	$ 3.10	$24.87	$1,115.30
13	806.65	695.79	2.75	75.00		18.23	2.75	12.13	
20	939.73	866.99	3.15	15.00	13.48	21.72	4.23	10.16	5.00
27	1,210.28	761.18	2.95	45.00	17.90	17.25	3.85	14.15	348.00
Totals	4,897.86	3,062.16	11.94	185.00	46.48	73.61	13.93	61.31	1,468.30
May 4	1,008.21	854.10	3.82	40.00	18.43	22.74	4.12		65.00
11	788.82	710.40	2.78	32.00		19.40	3.79	20.45	

Year-to-Date Financial Record   Year _____

RECEIPTS		Apr.	May	June	July	Aug.	Sept.	Oct.	Nov.	Dec.	Jan.	Feb.	Mar.
1. Tithe	Bud.	2,919	5,838	9,487	12,406	16,055	18,973	21,892	25,541	28,460	31,379	35,028	37,946
	Act.	3,062	5,619	9,291	12,192	15,881	18,765	22,113	27,310				
2. Junior Church	Bud.	13	26	38	51	64	75	88	101	113	126	139	150
	Act.	12	24	36	47	56	74	92	113				
3. Interest	Bud.	0	0	0	13	13	25	25	25	38	38	38	50
	Act.	0	0	11	11	11	24	24	24				
4. Easter—Thanksgiving Offering	Bud.	1,000	1,000	1,000	1,000	1,000	1,000	1,000	2,000	2,000	2,000	2,000	2,000
	Act.	1,115	1,115	1,115	1,115	1,115	1,115	1,115	2,207				
5. Building Fund	Bud.	200	400	600	800	1,000	1,200	1,400	1,600	1,800	2,000	2,200	2,400
	Act.	185	387	561	750	872	1,183	1,429	1,674				
6. Evangelism Offering	Bud.	166	332	498	664	830	995	1,161	1,327	1,493	1,659	1,825	1,990
	Act.	394	457	489	543	620	692	1,554	1,597				
7. Special Interest	Bud.	0	0	0	0	0	0	35	35	60	60	95	95
	Act.	5	5	5	20	20	20	55	55				
8. Sunday School	Bud.	137	274	411	548	685	823	960	1,097	1,234	1,371	1,508	1,645
	Act.	74	201	313	479	572	803	945	1,104				
9. NYI	Bud.	33	67	100	133	167	200	233	267	300	333	367	400
	Act.	14	49	79	117	143	187	202	244				
10. NWMS or Missions	Bud.	358	716	1,074	1,432	1,790	2,148	2,506	2,864	3,222	2,580	3,938	4,295
	Act.	61	427	469	1,210	1,416	2,174	2,545	2,913				
11. Day-Care Center	Bud.	1,125	2,250	3,375	4,500	5,625	6,750	7,875	9,000	10,125	11,250	12,375	13,500
	Act.	1,319	2,416	3,394	4,312	5,117	6,410	7,613	9,241				
12. Nonbudget Items	Bud.	0	0	0	0	0	0	0	0	0	0	0	0
	Act.	0	10	10	43	43	43	62	74				
13.	Bud.												
	Act.												
Total	Bud.	5,951	10,903	16,596	21,547	27,229	32,189	37,175	43,857	48,845	53,796	59,513	64,471
	Act.	6,241	10,710	15,773	20,839	25,866	31,490	37,749	46,556				

Year-to-Date Financial Record

DISBURSEMENTS		Apr.	May	June	July	Aug.	Sept.	Oct.	Nov.	Dec.	Jan.	Feb.	Mar.
1. Local Operating Fund	Bud.	2,131	4,262	6,392	8,523	10,654	12,785	14,916	17,047	19,178	21,309	23,440	25,570
	Act.	1,657	4,076	6,215	8,374	9,785	12,423	15,712	18,421				
2. Denominational Budgets by Church	Bud.	774	1,548	2,322	3,096	3,870	4,643	5,417	6,191	6,965	7,739	8,513	9,286
	Act.	1,889	2,496	3,103	3,710	4,317	4,924	5,531	7,230				
3. Building Fund & Debt Red.	Bud.	315	630	945	1,260	1,575	1,890	2,205	2,520	2,835	3,150	3,465	3,780
	Act.	315	630	945	1,260	1,575	1,890	2,205	1,520				
4. Building Maintenance	Bud.	158	317	475	633	791	950	1,108	1,266	1,425	1,583	1,741	1,900
	Act.	143	143	198	230	610	620	798	910				
5. Special Evangelism	Bud.	200	400	600	800	1,000	1,200	1,400	1,600	1,800	2,000	2,200	2,400
	Act.	258	258	258	317	367	561	1,560	1,625				
6. Special Interests	Bud.	0	0	0	0	0	0	35	35	60	60	85	95
	Act.	5	5	5	20	20	20	55	55				
7. Sunday School	Bud.	137	274	411	548	685	823	960	1,097	1,234	1,371	1,508	1,645
	Act.	84	324	393	482	705	820	1,003	1,088				
8. NYI	Bud.	33	67	100	133	167	200	233	267	300	333	367	400
	Act.	37	41	52	67	112	125	216	231				
9. NWMS or Missions	Bud.	358	716	1,074	1,432	1,790	2,148	2,506	2,864	3,222	3,580	3,938	4,295
	Act.	76	398	764	1,203	1,472	2,148	2,506	2,751				
10. Designated Funds	Bud.	0	0	0	0	200	200	200	200	200	200	200	200
	Act.	0	0	0	0	200	200	200	200				
11. Day-Care Center	Bud.	1,125	2,250	3,375	4,500	5,625	6,750	7,875	9,000	10,125	11,250	12,375	13,500
	Act.	743	2,019	2,711	3,987	4,973	6,400	7,842	8,762				
12.	Bud.												
	Act.												
13. Held in Reserve	Bud.	117	234	350	467	584	700	817	934	1,050	1,167	1,284	1,400
	Act.	117	234	350	467	584	700	817	934				
Total	Bud.	5,348	10,698	16,044	21,392	26,941	32,289	37,672	43,021	48,394	53,742	59,126	64,471
	Act.	5,324	10,624	14,994	20,117	24,720	30,832	38,445	44,727				

Requisition to Church Treasurer

Requisition No. _____ Amount $_____ Date _____

Pay to the order of _____

The sum of _____ dollars

Charge to:

1. Local Operational
   Fund
   A. _____ _____
   B. _____ _____
   C. _____ _____
2. Denominational
   Budgets
   _____ _____
   _____ _____
3. Building Fund and
   Debt Reduction
   _____ _____
4. Building
   Maintenance
   A. Current
   _____ _____
   B. Capital
   _____ _____
5. Evangelism
   _____ _____
   _____ _____
   _____ _____
   _____ _____

6. Special Interest
   _____ _____
   _____ _____
7. Sunday School ...... _____
8. NYI .... _____
9. NWMS .... _____
10. Designated Funds
    _____ _____
    _____ _____
11. _____ _____
For:

Signed: _____

Reference Notes

Chapter 1:

1. George R. Terry and Roger H. Hermanson, *Principles of Management* (Homewood, Ill.: Learning Systems Co., 1974), p. 1.

2. As quoted in a syllabus prepared by "Men in Action," Coral Gables, Fla.

Chapter 2:

1. As quoted in a syllabus prepared by "Men in Action," Coral Gables, Fla.

2. *Ibid.* 3. *Ibid.* 4. *Ibid.*

5. Robert Townsend, *Up the Organization* (Greenwich, Conn.: Fawcett Publications, Inc., 1971), p. 111.

Chapter 3:

1. R. Alec MacKensie, *The Time Trap* (New York: AMACOM, A Division of American Management Association, Inc., 1972), p. 113.

2. *Ibid.* 3. *Ibid.*, p. 114. 4. *Ibid.*, p. 115.

5. Quoted in *Nation's Business*, April, 1956.

6. MacKensie, *Time Trap*, p. 116.

7. Olan Hendrix, *Management and the Christian Worker* (Manila, Philippines: Christian Literature Crusade International, 1972), p. 124.

8. As quoted in a syllabus prepared by "Men in Action."

Chapter 4:

1. As quoted in a syllabus prepared by "Men in Action."

2. *Ibid.* 3. *Ibid.*

4. Douglas McGregor, *The Human Side of Enterprise* (New York: McGraw-Hill Co., 1961).

Chapter 5:

1. Hendrix, *Management*, p. 76. 2. *Ibid.*

3. As quoted in a syllabus prepared by "Men in Action."

4. Hendrix, *Management*.

Chapter 6

1. Robert K. Bower, *Administering Christian Education* (Grand Rapids, Mich.: Wm. B. Eerdmans Pub. Co., 1967).

2. As quoted in a syllabus prepared by "Men in Action."